THE
VESELKA
COOKBOOK

THE
VESELKA
COOKBOOK

Recipes and Stories from the Landmark Restaurant

in New York's East Village

TOM BIRCHARD
with **NATALIE DANFORD**

THOMAS DUNNE BOOKS

ST. MARTIN'S PRESS  NEW YORK

THOMAS DUNNE BOOKS.
An imprint of St. Martin's Press.

www.thomasdunnebooks.com
www.stmartins.com

Design by Maggie Hoffman

Library of Congress Cataloging-in-Publication Data
Birchard, Tom.
    The Veselka cookbook : recipes and stories from the landmark restaurant in New York's
East Village / Tom Birchard with Natalie Danford. — 1st ed.
        p. cm.
    ISBN 978-0-312-38568-2
    1. Cookery, Ukrainian. 2. Veselka (Restaurant) I. Danford, Natalie. II. Title.
    TX723.3.B523 2009
    641.59477—dc22

                                                                        2009024680

First Edition: November 2009

10 9 8 7 6 5 4 3 2 1

To the memory of

Wolodymyr Darmochwal,

founder of Veselka

CONTENTS

ACKNOWLEDGMENTS

First of all, I'd like to thank my collaborator, Natalie Danford, without whose help this book would not have been possible. Natalie was able magically to absorb the culture and cuisine of Veselka and put it into words more eloquently than I would have been able. Working with her was a total pleasure and I am forever grateful for all of her help.

I'd like to thank Lisa Straub, Veselka's pastry chef, who not only wrote up her own recipes for the many baked items she creates for Veselka but was instrumental in collecting all the recipes in this book, the vast majority of which appear here in written form for the first time. Lisa did an incredible job of making "a pinch of this and a pinch of that" concrete, and she handled much of the grunt work. I don't think I can overstate what a big help she was. My thanks, also, to Lucy Baker, who tested every recipe in this book, many of them twice and some three times, and patiently went over any adjustments and came up with her own suggestions for giving home cooks the tools for making the most Veselka-like dishes possible in their own kitchens.

Thanks, also, to editor Diana Szu, who gave this project a great deal of attention and unflagging enthusiasm. It feels almost strange to thank Angela Miller for serving as my agent on this book, as she's also a friend. Our casual meeting on a Vermont bike ride several years ago has proven extremely fortuitous. I'm so glad that she came up with the idea of a Veselka cookbook and encouraged me to do it. Nadea Mina contributed great ideas and thoughtful suggestions from the publicity end, and copy editor Leah Stewart cleaned it all up and made me look smart. My thanks to everyone at Thomas Dunne Books/St. Martin's Press for their hard work.

Of course, I am eternally grateful to the late Wolodymyr Darmochwal, the original owner of Veselka, for letting me work there and for founding such a unique restaurant. I'm very indebted to my son Jason Birchard, the next generation at Veselka and the third generation of the Darmochwal family to run the restaurant, and to Mykola and Zoriana Darmochwal, for working with me and maintaining the family connection and for their contributions to this book and especially their expertise on Ukrainian traditions and home cooking. Jason began working at Veselka when he was only fourteen years old and has been putting his heart and soul into it ever since. I'm grateful to everyone who has been a part of the dedicated Veselka staff over the last fifty-five years. I'd especially like to acknowledge cooks Aleksandra Grabska and Malgorzata Sibilska, who have worked with me for well over twenty years and are the backbone of the Veselka kitchen, as well as Gerhard Waldman, who recently retired after serving ably as Veselka's manager for many years. I've also enjoyed working with Julian Baczynsky for more than thirty years as he has supplied us with kielbasa and contributed in so many other ways to Veselka.

I'd also like to thank all the people who were interviewed for this book and graciously gave their time and energy to the project. I'm amazed, time and time again, at how personally connected everyone seems to feel to Veselka. Many thanks to Julian Baczynsky (again), Mort Zachter, Andy Lastowecky, Dona McAdams, Mark Russell, Penny Arcade, Tim Miller, and Arnie Charnick.

Bokek Ryzinski designed and built the current incarnation of Veselka and did a wonderful job of keeping the feel of the original while also updating the physical space. William Hellow has been Veselka's graphic designer since 1996 and not only designed our menus but is a true renaissance man with an extraordinary eye who has helped with lighting design and many other visual aspects of the restaurant. Ben Fink contributed most of the beautiful photographs in this book, and Petro R. Stawnychy, chair of Plast's National Executive Board, kindly allowed us to use the group's logo.

Finally, I'm so lucky to have a family that supports me, including not only Jason, who works side-by-side with me, but also my son Tom Jr., his wife, Sonja, and their children, Tyler and Serena (my beautiful grandchildren), and my children Kristen, Todd, and Sara. My wonderful wife Sally's unconditional love gives me so much strength and comfort that all things seem possible.

THE
VESELKA
COOKBOOK

This is the earliest known picture of Wolodymyr Darmochwal and the newsstand and candy shop he opened in 1954, Veselka. I'm not sure exactly when this was taken, but it appears to be sometime around 1960. *(Mykola Darmochwal)*

INTRODUCTION

I have a confession to make: I'm not Ukrainian. Actually, it's more accurate to say I wasn't *born* Ukrainian. In the more than forty years that I've worked at Veselka, a homey Ukrainian restaurant in New York's East Village, I've adopted the Ukrainian community, and the community has adopted me. I speak the language, if imperfectly. I serve the foods. I know the traditions. Today I'd say, and proudly, that I'm an honorary Ukrainian. It's funny, given what a big part of my life Veselka has become, that I don't clearly recall my first sight of what was then a humble lunch counter with a few tables and chairs. I have to admit that what I remember best was that I was actually slightly underwhelmed by the place. The space was small, and it was far from fancy. Like the neighborhood, it had a slightly dilapidated edginess to it. I was a suburban kid, and I wasn't used to an urban landscape. This was "the store"? My then-girlfriend's father, Wolodymyr Darmochwal, and her mother, Olha, had opened Veselka (which means "rainbow" in Ukrainian) as a newsstand and candy store in 1954, and they spent a lot of time discussing it. Though they lived in New Jersey, Wolodymyr rented an apartment across the street to keep a close eye on it. In my mind, it had been blown up into something bigger than it was.

But very shortly I found myself drawn to Veselka just as they were. I nurtured a real fascination with the Ukrainians who gathered there—everyone from kids coming down after Plast scouting activities upstairs to weary-looking workers to men and women in their later years who had lived in the United States for decades but never learned English. A sophomore in college, I began working at Veselka part-time, and my affection for its clientele continued to grow.

Here are two menus from previous versions of Veselka. The menu on the left dates back to 1960; the menu on the right was introduced in 1978.

I wasn't just interested in the people at Veselka, either. I found I loved the food served there, too. I'd grown up in New Jersey, in a typical suburban American household where the appearance of garlic or even a large amount of salt was highly unusual. To my underdeveloped taste buds, the hearty, strongly flavored Ukrainian specialties were brand-new, and pretty addictive. I discovered pierogi and borscht, kielbasa and cabbage soup.

The neighborhood surrounding Veselka had its own special allure. Manhattan wasn't nearly as neat and well-manicured in those days as it is now, and Veselka sat in the middle of a tight-knit Ukrainian immigrant community that was just displaying its first glimmer of gentrification. The phrase "East Village" was coined right around the same time—until then, this was just part of the Lower East Side, with all that that implied: immigrants living a little outside of mainstream American culture.

Indeed, in those days I stuck out like a sore thumb at Veselka, because I was the only person in the place who wasn't Ukrainian. Some older Ukrainian women were especially hard on me. I remember a group of them who used to come in and turn up their noses and say something in Ukrainian to Wolodymyr. Only later, when I'd learned Ukrainian myself, did I realize what they'd been saying all those times as I nodded and smiled naively in response was "He's not one of us." For his part, Wolodymyr did his best to turn me into an honorary Ukrainian, taking me to concerts and poetry readings and folk dancing performances and teaching me my first Ukrainian words.

Wolodymyr passed away in 1975, and though by then my relationship with his daughter was coming to an end, I was thoroughly enmeshed in the business of Veselka. I took over the restaurant at that point, and I often wonder what Wolodymyr would think if he could see it today. He wouldn't recognize the physical plant—though Veselka still sits on the same corner of 9th Street and Second Avenue, I rebuilt it from the bottom up when I renovated in 1996.

The East Village neighborhood around Veselka would be unrecognizable to him, too. When he passed away, New York City was at a low point, and heroin had hit this neighborhood hard. He'd be astonished that apartments on Veselka's funky block routinely sell for over a million dollars and now constitute some of the most sought-after real estate in the city. As a resident of

This article and photo appeared in a local Polish-language newspaper in 1981. That's me in the middle, with the moustache. To my left is a Ukrainian man who worked at Veselka for many years—one of two full-time jobs he held. I'm not sure who the woman to my right is—possibly the journalist who wrote the article.

Veselka has stood on the corner of East 9th Street and Second Avenue for more than fifty years. The photo on the left was taken around 1967, while the one on the right shows Veselka today. *(Photo left, Mykola Darmochwal; photo right, Sally Haddock)*

the East Village as well as a business owner, sometimes I have a hard time believing it myself.

What would amaze Wolodymyr most is that the restaurant is open twenty-four hours a day now, and is almost always crowded. When the original Veselka had even a half-dozen customers, he'd grow jittery and nervous and start moving around very briskly. Now a "busy day" means we've served over 1,000 people. I think he'd be proud to see what a success Veselka is, and I know he'd be very pleased that we still have plenty of Ukrainian specialties on the menu. He took his Ukrainian heritage very seriously, and I'm pleased, too, that we're able to carry on that tradition.

I'm even more pleased that it has become, in a way, my own tradition. I feel so grateful to have been associated with Veselka for as long as I have, and to have found a place for myself in both the Ukrainian community of New York City and in the East Village neighborhood at large. I don't think there's a more diverse, exciting group of people in the world than the artists and eccentrics, the academics and working people, and, yes, a core group of Ukrainian-Americans, who live in the area and frequent Veselka. Not only have the restaurant's customers become like family to me, but my own family is involved in Veselka as well. My wife, Sally, is a veterinarian who has had a practice down the street for twenty-two years, and she pitches in with menu design and interior decorating and is a tireless publicist for the restaurant. Mykola, Wolodymyr's son, and Mykola's wife, Zoriana, remain close to Veselka and continue to contribute: Mykola recently computerized our accounting and cost control systems. Today, my eldest son, Jason (Wolodymyr's grandson), is the general manager at Veselka. I hope some day he'll take over the restaurant and be the third generation to run it.

I may have been slightly underwhelmed by Veselka upon first seeing it, but walking through the doors today never fails to make me smile. I'm not just an honorary Ukrainian—I'm an extraordinarily lucky honorary Ukrainian. I hope that reading this book will help you feel a little Ukrainian, too.

1
SOUPS

WHEREVER YOU GO, there is soup: Big, warm pots of soup can be found simmering on stoves in every country in the world. There's a reason for that. Soup is the original comfort food. It's digestible—didn't your mother serve you soup when you had an upset stomach?—and it's economical, too. Back in Ukraine, where food had to be stretched, especially during the long, harsh winters, soup was a lifesaver. So it's no surprise that soup has been offered at Veselka since its opening day. Long before *Seinfeld* made the soup guy famous, we were ladling it out by the gallon.

Soup is very forgiving, too. If you've never cooked a thing in your life, soup is the perfect place to start—it's impossible to get it wrong, and any misstep can be fixed. After you've made these recipes a few times, you should feel free to experiment with them. If you've got a handful of cooked rice, use that in place of barley, or add some leftover vegetables, as long as you think their taste will blend.

The only thing that soup *won't* forgive is low-quality ingredients. I don't believe in saving a dollar here and a dollar there; I think in the end you make more money with quality. So at Veselka, with soups and everything else, we go the extra mile. For example, lots of restaurants—and home cooks, too—make chicken soup using bones and necks and wings and backs, but we always start with whole chickens. That results in a rounder, less bitter flavor, and it also means that we then have lots of boiled chicken meat to shred back into the soup and to use in other recipes as well.

In general, at the restaurant we cook a lot of ingredients separately, then combine them into a single soup at the end. This gives us a little more control over the individual components of the soup. In the morning we get a little soup assembly line going with various pots bubbling on the stove. There is always one soup or another cooking in the Veselka kitchen, though we don't make each kind every day. We rotate them. Our various types of borscht are among the most popular, and we also sell Cabbage Soup, a Ukrainian favorite made with sauerkraut, that's no longer available in many places. And every day we make one special soup, usually something seasonal, like our Butternut Squash Soup. A person could live on soup for a long, long time, and this collection of soup recipes provides a great start.

A Bowl of Borscht

There has never been a day in Veselka's fifty years without borscht on the menu. You know that guy in the Dunkin' Donuts commercial who used to say, "Time to make the donuts"? Well, at Veselka the beginning of the week and the middle of the week are "time to make the borscht." We start with over 250 pounds of beets, which are simmered and then allowed to cool on the first day of preparation. Our cooks refer to the resulting ruby-red liquid as "beet water." The next day we make a rich beef stock, and on the third day we combine the various ingredients. That results in just enough soup to last half a week, and one day later we begin all over again.

Simply put, borscht is beet soup, but borscht is far from simple at Veselka. We serve five different kinds of borscht: our standard version (which uses meat broth), a vegetarian version, Christmas borscht with dumplings, cold borscht (in summer), and white borscht—a special traditional variation made sour with either sauerkraut or fermented wheat.

While borscht is served throughout Eastern Europe and is a staple of Jewish cuisine (the word *bors* means "soup" in Yiddish), it is believed to have originated in Ukraine, and no wonder. Ukraine has many fine qualities, but excellent weather is not one of them. However, root vegetables like beets grow easily in the region, along with cabbage, and root vegetables could be stored in cellars in the days before refrigeration. There is little in life as comforting as sitting down to a bowl of ruby red borscht—we can only imagine how lively and tempting that sight was to someone entering a third month of below-zero temperatures and frozen terrain, or alternately, how refreshing a bowl of cold borscht would have been on a hot summer day.

In modern-day New York City, we may have heat and air conditioning, but that doesn't make a steaming bowl of borscht any less tempting. Cold borscht makes an elegant starter to a formal meal, while to us, Christmas wouldn't be Christmas without a dish of clear borscht with dumplings. The recipes for borscht in this book have been tested and retested so that you can re-create Veselka's borscht at home, but I think almost any Veselka customer would agree that nothing beats a bowl of the real thing, eaten right here.

VESELKA'S FAMOUS BORSCHT

Makes about 2 quarts; 8 first-course or 4 to 6 main-course servings

Borscht is *Veselka: We serve 5,000 gallons of the stuff every year. While at Veselka we cook the beets and the meat on separate days, you can do it all at the same time, as long as you've got enough large pots to handle it all. None of the work is very time-consuming, although the individual components simmer for several hours, so you'll need to pick a time when you'll be home, though not necessarily in the kitchen. You can easily double or triple this recipe (again, as long as you have large enough pots). After all, at Veselka, we work with 250 pounds of beets at a time. And keep in mind that borscht, like most soups, freezes beautifully.*

The beets for our borscht are cooked in two separate batches: One batch is used to make "beet water," a kind of rich beet stock. The remaining beets are cooked and grated. The process may sound a little complicated when you read it, but after you follow the instructions once, the logic will become clear, and I'm convinced that it's this two-step process that lends our borscht its distinct taste and depth of flavor.

You won't taste the white vinegar much, by the way, but it helps the beets retain the beautiful red color that is their hallmark. Without it, your borscht may take on a brownish tinge. If you are very sensitive to the taste of vinegar, use the full amount to cook the beet water and the beets, but in step 7, add it to the soup in small amounts, tasting in between.

3 pounds (10 to 12) small beets, scrubbed
   thoroughly but *not* peeled

9 tablespoons white vinegar

One 2-pound boneless pork butt, halved

8 cups Beef Stock (page 33)

1 bay leaf

1 teaspoon whole allspice berries

1 tablespoon whole black peppercorns

3 large carrots, peeled and sliced

3 large celery stalks, sliced

1 small head of green cabbage (about ¾
   to 1 pound), shredded (about 4 cups)

2 medium Idaho potatoes, peeled and cut
   into ½-inch dice

One 15-ounce can lima beans, drained and
   rinsed

Salt

1. To make the "beet water," roughly chop 2 pounds of the beets (select the smaller ones), preferably in a food processor fitted with the metal blade. Place the chopped beets in a large stockpot. Add 10 cups of water and 1 tablespoon vinegar.

2. Place the stockpot over high heat and bring to a boil, then reduce the heat to low, and simmer for 2 hours. (If it seems like the liquid is evaporating too quickly, you may need to cover the pot partially with an offset lid.) The beets should be extremely soft and the liquid bright red.

3. Strain the liquid, pressing the cooked beets against the side of the strainer to extract as much liquid as possible. Discard the pulp or reserve to make Beet Salad (page 90). Set aside the beet water. You should have just about 4 cups.

4. Meanwhile, place the remaining 1 pound of whole beets in a separate large stockpot. Add water to cover and bring to a boil. Reduce the heat to low, and simmer until the beets are tender-firm, about 40 minutes. When the beets are cooked, add 1 tablespoon white vinegar and set them aside to cool.

5. When the whole cooked beets are cool enough to handle, peel them; the skins should slip off easily. Grate the peeled beets on the largest holes of a box grater or in a food processor fitted with the grating blade.

6. To make the broth, place the pork butt in a large stockpot and add the beef stock. If necessary, add a little more stock or water to cover. Add the bay leaf, allspice berries, and peppercorns. Bring to a boil, reduce the heat to low, and simmer until the meat is tender and beginning to fall apart, about 2 hours. Set the pork aside to cool. When the pork is cool enough to handle, remove it from the pot and cut the meat into ½-inch cubes. Strain the broth and discard the bay leaf, allspice berries, and peppercorns. Reserve the cubed meat and 4 cups of the broth.

7. To cook the vegetables, place the carrots and celery in a large stockpot and pour the reserved meat broth over them. Bring to a boil, reduce the heat, and simmer until the carrots and celery are just tender, about 8 minutes. Add the cabbage and potatoes and continue to cook until the potatoes and carrots are easily pierced with a pairing knife but keep their shape, 15 to 20 additional minutes. Add the lima beans and cook for 5 additional minutes, just to meld the flavors. Gradually add the remaining 7 tablespoons white vinegar, tasting between additions and stopping when the flavor is to your liking. Remove the soup from the heat and set aside.

8. To compose the soup, in a large soup pot combine the "beet water" and meat broth with the vegetables. Add the cubed pork and the grated beets. Stir to combine and bring to a simmer over low heat. Season to taste with salt and serve immediately.

Variation: We also serve Vegetarian Borscht at Veselka, which is a little lighter and can be a better choice than traditional meat-based borscht when it's being served as part of a multi-course meal. For Vegetarian Borscht, simply leave out the pork butt, bay leaf, allspice, berries, and peppercorns, and skip step 6. In step 7, cook the vegetables in water or Vegetable Stock (page 36).

COLD BORSCHT

Makes about 2 quarts; 8 first-course or 4 main-course servings

Cold beet soup is tangy and refreshing—it's perfect on a really hot, humid day. If you're serving this as the first course in a fancy meal, pour it into tall glasses rather than bowls. The color is gorgeous.

1 pound (about 3) beets, scrubbed thoroughly but *not* peeled

½ cup half-and-half

1 cup buttermilk

1 tablespoon sugar

2 teaspoons white vinegar

4 large eggs, hard-boiled

2 tablespoons chopped fresh dill

1 small cucumber, peeled and diced

1. To make the "beet water," chop the beets roughly and place them in a stockpot. Add water to cover, at least 8 cups.
2. Place the stockpot over high heat and bring to a boil, reduce the heat to low, and simmer for 2 hours. (If it seems like the liquid is evaporating too quickly, you may need to partially cover the pot with an offset lid.) The beets should be extremely soft and the liquid should be bright red.
3. Strain the liquid, pressing the cooked beets against the side of the strainer to extract as much liquid as possible. Discard pulp or reserve to make Beet Salad (page 90). Reserve 3 cups of the beet water and set aside to cool completely. (If you have any leftover beet water, you can reserve it for another use or simply discard it.)
4. When the beet water has cooled, whisk it with the half-and-half and buttermilk. Add the sugar and vinegar and whisk until the sugar is dissolved and all the ingredients are combined. Chill until serving time.
5. Peel and chop the hard-boiled eggs.
6. To serve the soup, ladle portions into individual soup bowls and garnish each bowl with a sprinkling of fresh dill, chopped hard-boiled egg, and diced cucumber.

WHITE BORSCHT

Makes 2½ quarts; 6 to 8 servings

This unusual soup is generally served on holidays. It has a somewhat tart taste similar to sourdough bread. At Veselka, we use sauerkraut juice, but in some parts of Eastern Europe grain is fermented (similar to a sourdough starter) to make white borscht, and white vinegar will work as well. Sour soup sounds odd, I know, but this is highly addictive.

6 cups Chicken Stock (page 35)

2 medium ham hocks

3 smoked pork ribs, optional

1 medium onion, minced

3 large carrots, chopped

4 celery stalks, chopped

2 bay leaves

2 whole allspice berries

¾ cup sour cream

4 tablespoons all-purpose flour

¾ cup sauerkraut juice, or 2 teaspoons white vinegar

1 tablespoon dried marjoram

1 teaspoon dried oregano

Salt

Freshly ground black pepper

3 medium Idaho potatoes, cooked, peeled, and chopped

4 large eggs, hard-boiled and coarsely chopped

1. Place the chicken stock, ham hocks, pork ribs, if using, onion, carrots, celery, bay leaves, and allspice berries in a medium stockpot. Add 2 cups water. Bring to a boil, then lower to a gentle simmer and cook over low heat for 40 minutes.

2. Remove the ham hocks and ribs, if using, and discard. Strain out the vegetables and discard.

3. In a small bowl, whisk together the sour cream and the flour until very smooth.

4. Return the stock to a boil and stir in the sour cream–flour mixture. Add about half the sauerkraut juice or vinegar, taste, and add additional sauerkraut juice or vinegar, if desired. Stir in the marjoram and oregano, then reduce the heat to low, and simmer, stirring frequently, for 15 minutes.

5. Season to taste with salt (depending on how salty your sauerkraut juice is, it may not need any additional salt) and pepper.

6. Ladle the soup into individual serving bowls and garnish each serving with a few cubes of cooked potato and a sprinkling of chopped hard-boiled egg. Serve hot.

CHICKEN NOODLE SOUP

Makes about 2 quarts; 6 servings

After borscht, chicken noodle is our most popular soup. On a cold day, a rainy day, or really any day at all when you need a bit of a lift, chicken noodle soup is ideal. Chicken soup also has amazing healing powers: It has been scientifically proven to help colds heal faster. You can make the soup in advance, but if you're going to freeze chicken noodle soup, thaw it and cook the noodles in the broth just before serving. At Veselka, we use a whole chicken to make our soup. Not only does this result in a richer, more balanced broth, but you then have cooked chicken that can be used in so many different ways—Chicken Salad (page 95), sandwiches, or just eaten plain.

One 3½-pound chicken

1 large onion, peeled

3 celery stalks, sliced

3 large carrots, sliced

3 leeks, halved lengthwise and thoroughly
  cleaned

Salt

3 cups fine egg noodles

¼ cup minced flat-leaf parsley,
  for garnish

1. Place the chicken, onion, celery, carrot, and leeks in a large stockpot and add water to cover, at least 10 cups. Place over high heat, bring to a boil, reduce the heat to low, and simmer, uncovered (though you may want to partially cover the pot with a lid to stop the stovetop from being splattered), until the chicken meat is falling off the bone, about 1 hour. Skim off the fat and foam from the surface occasionally.

2. Remove the pot from the heat with the chicken still in the broth and allow to cool to room temperature.

3. Remove the chicken from the pot. Pull any meat from the bone and shred into large, rough pieces. Strain the chicken stock. Discard the onion and leeks, but set aside the celery and carrots. (Don't worry about a stray piece of onion or leek making its way in as well.)

4. Return the stock to the pot. Bring to a boil, add salt to taste, and toss in the noodles. Stir and turn down the heat to a brisk simmer. Cook until noodles are tender but still have a little bite at the center, about 8 minutes.

5. Return the shredded chicken and the cooked carrots and celery to the pot. Cook just to meld flavors and until noodles are perfectly tender, about 3 additional minutes.

6. Divide the soup among soup bowls. Garnish with chopped parsley and serve immediately.

CABBAGE SOUP

Makes 2½ quarts; 6 to 8 servings

When I started working at Veselka in 1967, we had a lot of Ukrainian men who, frankly, intimidated me. They would come in late at night—sometimes a little tipsy—and eat traditional Ukrainian foods and smoke cigarettes, and they seemed like tough customers. (This was decades before New York City would outlaw cigarette smoking in bars and restaurants. In fact, when Veselka was a combination newsstand and restaurant, cigarettes were sold at the counter.) This cabbage soup was one of their favorite dishes. I had never heard of a soup made with sauerkraut at the time, but it has since become one of my favorites, too—the simple yet forceful flavor cannot be ignored. When I've eaten too much rich food for a few days or my palate feels jaded, I find a bowl of Cabbage Soup really wakes me up.

1 boneless pork butt (about 2 pounds), halved	3 cups sauerkraut, drained
1½ quarts Chicken Stock (page 35)	1 large Idaho potato, peeled and diced
3 whole allspice berries	3 celery stalks, minced (about 1 cup)
3 bay leaves	2 large carrots, minced (about 1 cup)
1 tablespoon dried marjoram	1 small onion, cut into medium dice

1. Place the pork butt in a large stockpot with the chicken stock, 4 cups water, the allspice berries, bay leaves, and marjoram. Bring to a boil, reduce the heat to low, and simmer, uncovered (though you may want to partially cover the pot with a lid to stop the stovetop from being splattered), until the meat is fully cooked, tender, and beginning to fall apart, about 2 hours.
2. Remove the meat from the pot and set aside to cool. Skim most of the fat from the stock, leaving a few "eyes" of fat for flavor. Strain out and discard the bay leaves and allspice berries. Leave the pot on the stove.
3. Stir in the sauerkraut and simmer for 20 additional minutes.
4. Add the potato and simmer for 5 minutes. Then add the celery, carrot, and onion and simmer for 10 additional minutes. Finally, cut the reserved meat into large cubes and add to soup. Simmer for 10 additional minutes, until the flavors have melded and potato is cooked through, then serve immediately.

THREE-BEAN CHILI

Serves 6 to 8

This chili is so hearty and filling that I wasn't sure whether to include it in this chapter, with soups, or to place it in the chapter with recipes for meat entrées. There is nothing dainty or timid about it. This chili also makes good use of canned beans, since cooking the three types of beans separately would be time-consuming. Look for a good brand, preferably organic, with little or no sodium, as we toss in the bean liquid for extra flavor. At Veselka we cook up a vat of caramelized onions every morning and just scoop from that all day long, but here I've amended our recipe slightly so that you cook the onion as part of the recipe.

2½ pounds 80 percent lean ground beef

1½ cups chopped onion (2 medium onions)

One 15-ounce can black beans

One 15-ounce can white beans

Two 15-ounce cans red kidney beans, rinsed
  and drained

2 cups ketchup

3 tablespoons ground coriander

3 tablespoons ground cumin

3 tablespoons dried oregano

2 tablespoons chili powder

3 tablespoons dried basil

1 tablespoon salt

2 tablespoons freshly ground black pepper

1. In a large stockpot, cook the beef and onions over medium heat, stirring occasionally, until the meat is fully cooked and the onions are browned.

2. Drain off and discard excess fat.

3. Add the beans and their canning liquid, and the drained kidney beans to the pot. Stir in the ketchup, coriander, cumin, oregano, chili powder, and basil. Bring to a boil, reduce the heat to low, and simmer, uncovered (though you may want to partially cover the pot with a lid to stop the stovetop from being splattered), until the chili is very thick, about 1½ hours.

4. Season with the salt and pepper and serve hot.

ROASTED VEGETABLE CHILI

Serves 8

This unusual chili with a mother lode of roasted vegetables is in heavy rotation among our soup specials in the summer. Roasting really brings out the sweetness of zucchini and egg-plant. You can adjust the ratio of vegetables and beans here if you like. Just be sure that you chop all the vegetables into roughly the same size, otherwise small pieces will burn before large pieces are cooked through in the oven.

¼ cup plus 1 tablespoon extra-virgin olive oil

2 medium zucchini, cut into ½-inch dice

2 medium yellow squash, cut into ½-inch dice

1 medium eggplant, cut into ½-inch dice

1 red bell pepper, seeded and cut into ½-inch dice

8 ounces button mushrooms, stemmed and quartered

1 large onion, cut into ½-inch dice

2 garlic cloves, minced

One 28-ounce can crushed tomatoes

One 15-ounce can white beans, drained and rinsed

One 15-ounce can black beans, drained and rinsed

2 teaspoons chili powder

2 teaspoons paprika

1 tablespoon ground cumin

1 teaspoon cayenne pepper

Salt

Freshly ground black pepper

1 bunch scallions, thinly sliced

¼ cup loosely packed cilantro leaves, optional

¼ cup shredded Vermont cheddar cheese, optional

1. Preheat oven to 400°F.

2. Line two jelly-roll pans with aluminum foil and coat each lightly with about 1 tablespoon of the olive oil. Combine the zucchini, yellow squash, eggplant, and bell pepper on one pan and spread the mushrooms on the other. Drizzle another tablespoon of olive oil over the vegetables on each pan, and roast in the preheated oven, stirring occasionally to keep from sticking, until the zucchini, squash, and eggplant are lightly browned, 15 to 20 minutes, and until the mushrooms have given up all of their liquid, about 25 minutes.

3. While the vegetables are roasting, in a large ovenproof stockpot or Dutch oven, sauté the onion and garlic in the remaining 1 tablespoon of olive oil until translucent, about 3 minutes.

4. Add the canned tomatoes, beans, chili powder, paprika, cumin, and cayenne. When the roasted vegetables are done, transfer them to the pot and lower the oven temperature to 350°F. Stir the vegetables into the chili, cover the pot with a lid, and transfer the pot to the 350°F oven. Roast the chili for 1 hour. Check occasionally and add a little water (or additional crushed tomatoes, if you prefer) if the chili seems to be getting too thick, but it should be nice and hearty. (You can also cook the chili on the stovetop for 45 minutes to 1 hour, but keep a close eye on it to be sure the bottom doesn't scorch, which can happen easily.)

5. Taste the chili and adjust the seasoning with salt and pepper, if necessary. Spoon the chili into individual bowls and top each serving with a sprinkling of scallions and cilantro leaves and some cheddar cheese, if using. Serve immediately.

SPLIT PEA SOUP

Makes 2½ quarts; 6 to 8 servings

On a dreary fall day in New York City, nothing cheers me up like a bowl of dense, slightly chunky split pea soup. Unlike a lot of split pea soup recipes, ours doesn't include any pork, so it's great for vegetarians, too. Grate the carrots and celery on the smallest holes of a box grater, or mince them thoroughly in a food processor.

2 tablespoons unsalted butter

2 large carrots, minced

3 stalks celery, minced

3 cups dried split peas, rinsed and picked over

6 cups Vegetable Stock (page 36)

Salt

Freshly ground black pepper

1. Melt the butter in a large stockpot over low heat.

2. Add the carrot and celery and cook, stirring occasionally, until they have softened, about 8 minutes.

3. Stir in the split peas, stock, and 2 cups water. Bring the soup to a boil, reduce the heat to low, and simmer, uncovered (though you may want to partially cover the pot with a lid to stop the stovetop from being splattered), until the peas are tender and dissolved, about 1 hour.

4. If you prefer a less chunky soup, stir in a little more water or stock. Season to taste with salt and a generous amount of pepper and serve hot.

LENTIL SOUP

Makes 2½ quarts; 6 to 8 servings

There's something special about lentils—even people who claim they don't like other legumes seem to like them. Lentils are great in soups, salads (see the Lentil Salad on page 91), and just about anything else. They're also supereasy to prepare—if you've never cooked a thing in your life, you'll be able to make this soup.

2 tablespoons unsalted butter

1 large carrot, grated

2 celery stalks, minced

1 small Vidalia onion, minced

3 cups lentils, rinsed and picked over

6 cups Vegetable Stock (page 36)

Salt

Freshly ground black pepper

1. Melt the butter in a large stockpot over low heat.

2. Add the carrot, celery, and onion and cook, stirring occasionally, until they have softened, about 8 minutes.

3. Add the lentils, vegetable stock, and 2 cups water. Simmer over low heat, uncovered (though you may want to partially cover the pot with a lid to stop the stovetop from being splattered), until the lentils are tender, about 1 hour. Add small amounts of water in order to keep the lentils covered while they simmer, if necessary. Season to taste with salt and pepper and serve hot.

MUSHROOM BARLEY SOUP

Serves 8

This is a rib-sticking vegetarian soup that, with a slice or two of good bread, makes a meal. To cook the barley, start with about ¾ cup dried barley, and stir it into 2 cups boiling water. Cover the pot and simmer for about 30 minutes. You want the barley to still be a little chewy—that's one of its finest qualities. And, yes, we use a little canned mushroom soup as a shortcut at the restaurant, supplemented with lots of fresh mushrooms and other vegetables. That's how Veselka's founder, Wolodymyr Darmochwal, was making this soup when I came to work at the restaurant, and we've continued the tradition. If you like, you can leave it out, though the soup's flavor will be substantially different—taste it both before and after adding the canned soup the first time you make it and judge for yourself which is better. For the fresh mushrooms, you can include the upper part of the stems as well as the caps.

2 tablespoons unsalted butter

2 large carrots, minced

3 celery stalks, minced

5 cups minced white button mushrooms

6 cups Vegetable Stock (page 36)

One 10-ounce can cream of mushroom soup, optional

2 cups cooked barley

Freshly ground black pepper

1. Melt the butter in a large stockpot over low heat.

2. Add the carrot and celery and cook, stirring occasionally, until they have softened, about 8 minutes.

3. Add the mushrooms and vegetable stock. Bring to a boil, reduce the heat to low, and simmer, uncovered (though you may want to partially cover the pot with a lid to stop the stovetop from being splattered), for 30 minutes. Stir in the cream of mushroom soup, if using, and the barley. Season to taste with a generous amount of black pepper. Continue to cook until the flavors have combined, about 5 more minutes. Serve hot.

VEGETABLE SOUP

Makes 2½ quarts; 6 to 8 servings

Vegetable soup is a great way to get the five to seven servings of fruits and vegetables we're always hearing about into your daily diet. At Veselka, we use the combination given here, but feel free to use these as a mere guideline. If you have some nice-looking spinach or other greens, toss them in. The same goes for celery, turnips, potatoes, and so on. Even frozen vegetables will do in a pinch. Just be sure the vegetables are cut into pieces that are roughly the same size.

6 cups Vegetable Stock (page 36)

1 small onion, minced

2 large carrots, shredded on the smallest holes of a box grater

1½ cups chopped string beans

1½ cups chopped cauliflower florets

2 small Idaho potatoes, peeled and diced

1 cup peas (frozen peas are fine)

3 tablespoons unsalted butter

3 tablespoons all-purpose flour

Salt

Freshly ground black pepper

1. Combine the stock and all the vegetables in a medium stockpot. Bring to a boil, reduce the heat to low, and simmer, uncovered (though you may want to partially cover the pot with a lid to stop the stovetop from being splattered), until all the vegetables are tender, about 30 minutes.

2. While the soup is cooking, make a roux. In a small sauté pan, melt the butter, stir in the flour, and cook over low heat, whisking constantly, until the mixture is slightly golden and there are no lumps, about 3 minutes.

3. Whisk the roux into the soup. Season to taste with salt and pepper and serve hot.

BUTTERNUT SQUASH SOUP

Serves 6 to 8

This is one of our most popular seasonal soups, and it is in heavy rotation in the fall and winter, when bulbous butternut squash are widely available. Look for squash that are free of soft spots and feel heavy for their size. Like most soups, this benefits from being made in advance. If you're a real ginger fanatic, increase the fresh ginger to 2 tablespoons, or even 3.

3 tablespoons vegetable oil

2 medium butternut squash

1 large onion, chopped

2 garlic cloves, chopped

½ cinnamon stick

1 packed tablespoon dark brown sugar

1 tablespoon grated fresh ginger, plus
   additional if desired

6 cups Chicken Stock (page 35)

Salt

Freshly ground black pepper

2 tablespoons minced candied ginger

¼ cup chopped flat-leaf parsley

1. Preheat the oven to 375°F. Line a jelly-roll pan with a sheet of aluminum foil, coat with 1 tablespoon of the vegetable oil, and set aside.

2. With a large cleaver, split the squash lengthwise. Scoop out and discard the seeds and strings. Place the squash cut-side down on the prepared pan and roast until the squash is soft enough to pierce with a paring knife, about 1 hour. Set the squash aside to cool, and when it is cool enough to handle, remove the flesh from the peel and cut into 1-inch chunks. Set aside. Discard the peel.

3. In a medium stockpot or Dutch oven, heat the remaining 2 tablespoons of oil. Sauté the chopped onion until translucent, about 5 minutes. Add the garlic, cinnamon stick, brown sugar, and ginger and sauté for 1 additional minute.

4. Add the chopped cooked squash and the stock and simmer until the squash is very soft, about 20 minutes. Allow the soup to cool in the pot for about 15 minutes, then remove the cinnamon stick and purée the soup. (The best way to do this is with an immersion blender right in the pot, but if you don't have an immersion blender, carefully transfer the soup to a blender and purée in batches, then return it to the pot.)

5. Season the soup to taste with salt and pepper. Reheat the soup until it just begins to bubble, then thin with a little water if it seems too thick.

6. Ladle the hot soup into individual serving bowls and garnish each serving with a little candied ginger and chopped parsley. Serve immediately.

TOMATO RICE SOUP

Serves 6 to 8

In summer, and early fall, when we have access to an abundance of really good ripe toma-toes, we make this soup very frequently. The tomatoes should be juicy and ripe to the point of bursting. Don't even bother trying to make this with mealy winter tomatoes. If you do dis-cover at the end of step 2 that your tomatoes have not given you enough juice, you can sup-plement it with a little canned tomato purée, but if you are using super-ripe seasonal tomatoes that won't be necessary.

3½ pounds very ripe fresh tomatoes

6 cups Chicken Stock (page 35)

1 small onion

1 carrot

2 celery stalks

2 tablespoons sugar

1½ cups sour cream

2 tablespoons cornstarch

2 cups cooked short-grain white
  rice

Salt

Freshly ground black pepper

¼ cup chopped flat-leaf parsley

1. Remove the stem ends and quarter the tomatoes and purée them in a food pro-cessor fitted with the metal blade. Strain the resulting purée, pressing with a wooden spoon to extract as much juice as possible, and set the juice aside.

2. Transfer the tomato seeds and skin to a medium pot and place over low heat. Bring to a very gentle simmer, then strain again. You'll get a fair amount of ad-ditional juice this way. Combine it with the first batch of juice and set aside. Discard the seeds and skin. You should have about 3 cups of tomato juice.

3. Meanwhile, heat up the chicken stock in a large stockpot. Mince the onion, car-rot, and celery and add them to the chicken stock. Cook at a gentle simmer until the vegetables are soft, about 30 minutes.

4. Add the fresh tomato juice to the stock and bring to a boil.

5. When the stock is boiling, in a medium bowl combine the sour cream and corn-starch and whisk until the mixture is very smooth with no lumps.

6. Ladle out about ½ cup of the hot liquid and whisk it into the sour cream–cornstarch mixture. Return the sour cream mixture to the pot and bring to a boil, then reduce to a simmer.

7. Simmer for an additional 15 minutes, stirring frequently. The soup should thicken nicely. Stir in the cooked rice (continue cooking for a minute or two if the rice was cold to make sure it heats through). Season to taste with salt and pepper and gradually add the sugar, if needed. (If your tomatoes are really ripe and sweet, you may not need any.) Garnish with chopped parsley and serve hot.

COLD CUCUMBER SOUP

Serves 4 to 6

This is another one of our popular seasonal soups. A bowl of cold soup—made with vegetables or even fruit—is a refreshing treat in the summer. This couldn't be easier to assemble.

4 seedless cucumbers

1 large garlic clove

3 tablespoons chopped fresh dill, plus more
   for garnish

2½ cups buttermilk

1 cup half-and-half

2 teaspoons salt

1 teaspoon freshly ground black pepper

2 teaspoons Dijon mustard

1. Peel 3 of the cucumbers. Chop the peeled cucumbers into 3 or 4 pieces. Working in batches, place them in the bowl of a food processor fitted with the metal blade, along with the garlic. Purée until smooth.

2. In a large bowl, combine the puréed cucumber, dill, buttermilk, half-and-half, salt, pepper, and mustard. Whisk together until thoroughly combined.

3. Cut the remaining unpeeled cucumber into small dice. Serve the soup chilled, sprinkled with the diced cucumber and a little chopped dill for garnish.

BEEF STOCK

Makes about 2 quarts

To make a classic French-style beef stock, you should roast the bones and the onion, garlic, and carrots to draw out their flavor. If you're in a hurry, skip that step and roast those items right in the stockpot over medium heat, stirring frequently to keep things from sticking to the bottom, for 15 minutes or so before you add the water. (Then again, if you're really in a hurry, you probably shouldn't start this recipe at all, as it requires 4 to 5 hours of simmering.) A good butcher can provide you with bones, or you can save bones in the freezer until you have enough. Shank bones are always a good choice for the stock pot. In a pinch, you can use canned beef broth, but it will never taste as good as a made-from-scratch stock like this, and you can make this in big batches and freeze it almost indefinitely.

3½ pounds beef bones

1 onion, peeled and roughly chopped

2 garlic cloves, peeled

2 large carrots, peeled and roughly chopped

2 celery stalks, roughly chopped

1 tomato, halved

1 bay leaf

1 teaspoon dried thyme

4 sprigs parsley

6 whole black peppercorns

1 teaspoon salt

1. Preheat the oven to 450°F. Place the bones, onion, garlic, and carrots in a roasting pan and roast, uncovered, in the preheated oven, turning the bones a few times, until browned, about 30 minutes.

2. Skim off the fat from the roasting pan. Transfer the roasted bones and vegetables to your largest soup or stockpot. Add about ½ cup water to the roasting pan. Using a wooden spoon or a spatula, dislodge any bits that have stuck to the bottom of the pan, then pour this liquid into the soup or stockpot.

3. Add the celery, tomato, bay leaf, thyme, parsley, peppercorns, and salt. Add cold water to fill the pot, at least 8 cups.

4. Cover the pot and place it over high heat. Bring to a boil, then reduce the heat to low, and simmer, uncovered (though you may want to partially cover the pot with a lid to stop the stovetop from being splattered), skimming occasionally

during the first 30 minutes, until the liquid has turned a deep, rich brown, 4 to 5 hours.

5. Strain the stock and discard the solids. (You may want to wait until the stock has cooled somewhat for safety's sake.) Refrigerate the stock, then skim off some or all of the fat that accumulates on the surface.

CHICKEN STOCK

Makes about 2 quarts

Though the two tend to get conflated, there is a difference between chicken broth and chicken stock. Stock is, by definition, made with bones and vegetables, not with meat. What we use for all our preparations at Veselka is actually a chicken broth. If you like, you can substitute backs, wings, necks, and feet for the meaty chicken parts in the recipe below and make a true stock (though I wouldn't eat it plain as soup—it doesn't have the rounded flavor a true broth does). You can also use the carcasses of roasted birds from which you've already eaten all the meat. Or you can use a combination of all three of these things, or even strain a little Chicken Noodle Soup (page 18) and use that (without the noodles, obviously). If you do use meaty chicken parts, be sure to reserve the cooked chicken and use it for sandwiches, in stir-fries, or to make Chicken Salad (page 95). Extra chicken stock can be poured into heavy-duty ziplock bags and frozen.

3½ pounds chicken parts

1 onion (no need to peel it)

2 large carrots, peeled and roughly chopped

2 celery stalks, roughly chopped

1 bay leaf

6 whole black peppercorns

1 teaspoon salt

1. Place the chicken parts in your largest soup or stockpot. Add cold water to fill the pot, at least 8 cups.

2. Add the remaining ingredients to the pot.

3. Cover the pot and place it over high heat. Bring to a boil, then reduce the heat to low and simmer, uncovered (though you may want to partially cover the pot with a lid to stop the stovetop from being splattered), skimming occasionally during the first 30 minutes, until the liquid has turned a deep golden yellow color, 1 to 1½ hours. (It's better to overdo it than to stop too soon—you can't really overcook chicken stock.)

4. Strain the stock. Set aside the cooked chicken for later use. Discard any other solids. (You may want to wait until the stock has cooled somewhat for safety's sake.) Refrigerate the stock, then skim off some or all of the fat that accumulates on the surface.

VEGETABLE STOCK

Makes about 2 quarts

We use vegetable stock in our vegetarian soups. In a pinch you can use water in place of vegetable stock, but the stock gives a more nuanced flavor, plus, it's very good for you. You could use almost any vegetables you have on hand here, with the exception of very strong-tasting vegetables such as cabbage or broccoli. Vegetable stock doesn't need to cook nearly as long as chicken stock. A mere 30 minutes of simmering should be enough to draw all the flavor out of your vegetables. This stock, too, freezes very nicely.

2 onions, peeled and halved

4 carrots, peeled and chopped

4 celery stalks, chopped

1 parsnip, peeled and chopped

12 sprigs flat-leaf parsley

1 bay leaf

6 whole black peppercorns

1 teaspoon salt

1. Place all the ingredients in your largest soup or stockpot. Add cold water to fill the pot, at least 8 cups.
2. Cover the pot and place it over high heat. Bring to a boil, then reduce the heat to low, and simmer, uncovered (though you may want to partially cover the pot with a lid to stop the stovetop from being splattered), skimming occasionally during the first 15 minutes, until the vegetables are very soft, about 30 minutes.
3. Strain the stock and discard the solids.

2

STUFFED DELIGHTS:
PIEROGI, BLINTZES, AND MORE

IN THE FIRST HALF of the twentieth century, Ukraine was not an easy place to live. The harsh climate and often difficult political situation over the years shaped the Ukrainian diet into a regime heavily reliant on foods like cabbage and potatoes.

In order to provide variety, Ukrainians have excelled at composing dishes out of the same few ingredients. One of the main techniques Ukrainians developed, consciously or not, to make things a little more interesting is wrapping foods. At Veselka we continue that tradition with inexpensive, belly-filling food that warms and comforts. Stuffed cabbage (meat or vegetarian) and pierogi, sometimes referred to as *varenyky*, are two of our most popular—and most traditionally Ukrainian—dishes.

Assembling these dishes does take a little extra effort. You'll be rolling and pinching and sealing. These are good opportunities to get children comfortable in the kitchen—their nimble little fingers seem to be particularly adept at this kind of work.

In any case, whether you enlist an army or you're an army of one making these dishes, the results are well worth the time they take, and all stuffed foods can be assembled in advance and frozen. There's little more pleasurable than pulling a tray of frozen stuffed cabbage out of your freezer, allowing it to thaw, and then heating it up in the oven. It's good, homemade food at your hand, at any time.

POTATO PIEROGI

Makes 65 to 70 pierogi; 8 to 10 servings

We never paid much attention to the whole low-carb craze at Veselka. Not only is the restaurant not susceptible to fads, but eating that way would have meant giving up potato pierogi, and there's no way we could do that. Our nimble-fingered cooks make as many as 3,000 pierogi every single day. This recipe doesn't make quite that many, but it does yield a large amount. You could halve the recipe, but instead I recommend making the full amount and freezing half. Frozen pierogi can be dropped directly into boiling water for cooking; there's no thawing required. You can also refrigerate the dough for a day or two, so you can make the pierogi in a couple batches. Or you could just eat more than the seven pierogi that we consider a single serving at Veselka in one sitting—not exactly punishment.

PIEROGI WRAPPERS

1 large egg yolk

1 cup whole milk

1 tablespoon vegetable oil

3¼ cups all-purpose flour

TO ASSEMBLE

2 large egg whites

All-purpose flour, as needed

Sour cream, for serving

TOPPING AND FILLING

4 tablespoons unsalted butter

5 cups finely chopped onion

4 cups mashed potatoes (leftovers are fine)

4 ounces farmer's cheese

2 teaspoons salt

¼ teaspoon freshly ground black pepper

1. To make the wrappers, in a small bowl, combine the egg yolk, milk, ½ cup water, and the vegetable oil. Whip with a fork for 1 minute. Place the flour in a large bowl. Make a well in the center and pour in the wet ingredients, about one-third at a time, using your fingers or a fork to incorporate the wet ingredients between additions.

2. When you have added all the wet ingredients, use your hands to fold the dough together. If it seems too sticky, add a little more flour, about 1 teaspoon at a time to avoid making it too dry.

3. Transfer the dough to a lightly floured board and knead for 3 minutes. Again, add very small amounts of flour if the dough is too sticky to knead. When the dough is smooth and thoroughly amalgamated, form it into a ball, transfer it to a small bowl, cover with plastic wrap, and refrigerate for 20 minutes. Clean and dry your work surface.

4. While the dough is chilling, prepare the topping and filling. Melt the butter in a large sauté pan, then add the onions and sauté over medium heat, stirring occasionally, until browned, about 10 minutes.

5. In a large bowl, combine ¾ cup of the cooked onions, the mashed potatoes, farmer's cheese, salt, and pepper. Set aside at room temperature. Reserve the remaining onions for the topping.

6. When you are ready to roll the dough, in a small bowl combine the 2 egg whites with 2 tablespoons water and set it to the side of your work surface. You will also need a pastry brush, a rolling pin, a teaspoon (the table kind, not a measuring spoon), a fork, and a round cookie cutter about 2¾ inches in diameter (a jar lid or juice glass will also work). Set aside a floured jelly-roll pan, platter, or cutting board for the finished pierogi as well.

7. Divide the dough into 3 sections. Place 1 section on the work surface, well-floured, and roll out to ¹⁄₁₆ inch. Cut circles of dough with the cookie cutter. Place a heaping teaspoon of the filling in the center of each circle, leaving an empty margin. Brush some of the egg white mixture on half of the outer edge of the circle, and then fold the dough over into a half-moon shape. Crimp the edges with your fingers or with a small fork.

8. As you finish, transfer each pierogi to the floured board or platter. Do not stack them. Repeat with remaining dough and filling.

9. Fill a large stockpot about three-quarters full with salted water and bring to a rolling boil. Using a slotted spoon or skimmer, lower the pierogi, three or four at a time, into the boiling water and cook for 4 minutes. Remove with a slotted spoon, drain, and transfer to a serving platter. Repeat with the remaining pierogi, allowing the water to return to a full boil each time.

PIEROGI FILLINGS

Makes enough filling for 65 to 70 pierogi; 8 to 10 servings

Potato Pierogi are our most popular type and the most common type of pierogi throughout Eastern Europe, where pierogi originated. But you can stuff pierogi with almost any substance that will cook to the right consistency—soft, fairly smooth, and not too wet. Pierogi fillings should be strongly seasoned, too, as they are eaten in such small amounts. Each of these recipes will make enough filling for one batch of pierogi wrappers, prepared as above, but they are all easy to cut in half, so you can make one batch of a couple of different kinds of pierogi. As with the Potato Pierogi, you can boil these or pan-fry them. Either way, top with lots of browned onion and some sour cream.

CHEESE PIEROGI FILLING

3 cups farmer's cheese

2 large eggs

4 tablespoons sugar, or more to taste

2 tablespoons all-purpose flour

2 teaspoons salt

1. Place all the ingredients in a medium bowl.

2. Stir vigorously with a fork to combine. Set aside at room temperature.

SPINACH AND CHEESE PIEROGI FILLING

1 tablespoon unsalted butter

2 tablespoons chopped onion

Three 10-ounce boxes frozen chopped
  spinach, thawed and squeezed dry

2 cups farmer's cheese

2 teaspoons freshly ground black pepper

2 teaspoons salt

1. To make the filling, melt the butter in a medium sauté pan and cook the onion in the butter over medium heat until it is a dark, rich brown, about 10 minutes. (If you are making and serving the pierogi on the same day, you may want to cook the onion for the topping at the same time using about 4 cups. Then simply reserve 2 tablespoons of cooked onion for the filling and use the rest for the topping.)

2. Place the 2 tablespoons cooked onion and the remaining filling ingredients in a medium bowl and stir vigorously with a fork to combine. Set aside at room temperature.

SAUERKRAUT AND MUSHROOM PIEROGI FILLING

8 cups roughly chopped button mushrooms

2 cups drained Sauerkraut (page 94)

2 tablespoons all-purpose flour

2 teaspoons freshly ground black pepper

1. Preheat the oven to 350°F. Spread the chopped mushrooms in a single layer on two half-sheet or jelly-roll pans and roast until the mushrooms are cooked and have given up their liquid and the liquid has evaporated, about 1½ hours. Remove and set aside to cool.

2. When the mushrooms have cooled, in a large bowl combine them with the sauerkraut, flour, and pepper (no salt, as the sauerkraut is salty) and toss to combine thoroughly.

ARUGULA AND GOAT CHEESE PIEROGI FILLING

1 tablespoon unsalted butter

¼ cup chopped onion

3 tightly packed cups arugula, chopped

2 cups goat cheese, at room temperature

1 cup cream cheese, at room temperature

2 teaspoons freshly ground black pepper

2 teaspoons salt

1. Melt the butter in a medium sauté pan and cook the onion in the butter over medium heat until it is a dark, rich brown, about 10 minutes. (If you are making and serving the pierogi on the same day, you may want to cook the onion for the topping at the same time. Then simply reserve ¼ cup of cooked onion for the filling and use the rest for the topping.)

2. Place the ¼ cup cooked onion and the remaining filling ingredients in a medium bowl and stir vigorously with a fork to combine. Set aside at room temperature.

SWEET POTATO PIEROGI FILLING

2 tablespoons unsalted butter

½ cup chopped onion

4 large sweet potatoes, boiled, peeled, and
   mashed

½ cup farmer's cheese

1 tablespoon all-purpose flour

2 teaspoons freshly ground black pepper

1. Melt the butter in a medium sauté pan and cook the onion in the butter over medium heat until it is a dark, rich brown, about 10 minutes. (If you are making and serving the pierogi on the same day, you may want to cook the onion for the topping at the same time using about 4½ cups. Then simply reserve ½ cup of cooked onion for the filling and use the rest for the topping.)

2. Place the ½ cup cooked onion and the remaining filling ingredients in a medium bowl and stir vigorously with a fork to combine. Set aside at room temperature.

MEAT PIEROGI FILLING

2 pounds beef roast, cut into 2-inch cubes

4½ cups Chicken Stock (page 35)

2 chicken breasts, 2 chicken thighs, and 2
   chicken legs (about 2 pounds total)

1 tablespoon unsalted butter

¼ cup chopped onion

1½ teaspoons freshly ground black pepper

¾ teaspoon salt

1. To make the filling, place the beef in a medium saucepan, add 2 cups of the chicken stock, and add cold water to cover, if necessary. Bring to a boil, reduce the heat, and simmer until tender, 45 minutes to 1 hour. Set aside to cool.

2. At the same time, place the chicken parts in another medium saucepan and pour over 2 cups of the chicken stock. Add cold water to cover, if necessary. Bring to a boil, reduce the heat, and simmer until the chicken is fully cooked, about 30 minutes. Drain and set aside to cool.

3. Meanwhile, melt the butter in a medium sauté pan and cook the onion in the butter over medium heat until it is a dark, rich brown, about 10 minutes. (If you are making and serving the pierogi on the same day, you may want to cook the onion for the topping at the same time using about 4¼ cups. Then simply reserve ¼ cup of cooked onion for the filling and use the rest for the topping.)

4. When the chicken has cooled, using your hands, pull the meat and the skin from the chicken bones. Discard the bones. Place the chicken meat, chicken skin, and cooked beef in a food processor fitted with the metal blade and grind to a paste. (Depending on the size of your processor, you may need to do this in batches.)

5. For the filling, in a medium bowl combine the cooked onion, the ground chicken and beef, pepper, and salt. Sprinkle on the remaining ½ cup chicken stock and mix to combine thoroughly. (Using your hands is best.)

HAM AND SWISS PIEROGI FILLING

2 cups shredded cooked ham

2 cups grated Swiss cheese

2 teaspoons freshly ground black pepper

2 teaspoons salt

2 tablespoons all-purpose flour

1 cup mashed potatoes (leftovers are fine)

1. In a large bowl, combine all the ingredients.

2. Knead the mixture with your hands until it is well incorporated.

The Pierogi Makers

In a basement room below Veselka sit four women, Ala, Maria, Danuta, and Maria, who are responsible for a large percentage of the restaurant's business: These women chat in Polish as they roll and stir and pinch for eight hours a day to feed the craving for pierogi that haunts so many of Veselka's customers. Since 1976, every single one of the upwards of 3,000 pierogi served daily at Veselka—these doughy stuffed dumplings from Eastern Europe are by far our most popular dish—have been made by hand. (Before then we experimented with machinery that occasionally jammed and sent pierogi flying through the air, even with thinned wonton skins, but nothing could ever match the quality of handmade pierogi.)

All four women—and all the pierogi makers we've employed in the past—learned from their mothers how to make the dumplings. Ala has been part of the Veselka pierogi team the longest, so long that she can't remember when she came to us. She also can't remember a time when making pierogi wasn't automatic. When I ask her how much filling goes into each pierogi, for example, she draws a blank. "I have a scale built into my hand." She shrugs.

The filling turns out to be a surprisingly large amount—about the size of a golf ball. Then again, all the amounts for making pierogi at the restaurant are large. Each day the pierogi makers mix up a batch of dough consisting of 50 pounds of flour, 60 egg yolks, 3 gallons of milk, and 2 cups of oil. (Don't worry—the recipe in this book has been cut down to a size manageable in home kitchens!) The dough is mixed in an industrial-size mixer to develop the gluten, then rolled first through a machine that looks like a gigantic pasta machine, then by hand with a rolling pin.

The pierogi makers then grasp their 2-inch round cutters—the same ones that we've had at the restaurant for more than thirty years—and, so quickly that you might miss it if you blink, they punch out the pierogi wrappers. One of those metal cutters was lost fifteen years ago, and Ala won't let me forget it.

"Take care of that better than you take care of your wife," she admonishes me when I dare to pick up one of the cutters. When the women leave at about 11:00 P.M., they hide the cutters.

Each circle is then wrapped around a clump of filling and stretched to cover it and simultaneously pinched to seal it. The traditional filling, and our best-seller, is an amalgam of mashed Idaho potatoes, farmer's cheese, and browned onions. The onions must be browned the same day they are used, which means every day for the pierogi makers begins with tears as they chop a minimum of ten large onions.

While potato remains our most popular pierogi filling, over the years Veselka has developed plenty of traditional (meat, spinach, cabbage) and new-fangled fillings. The latter have included broccoli and cheese, ham and cheese, arugula and goat cheese, sweet potato, cherry pierogi for Washington's Birthday, and apple-raisin pierogi by special request for loyal customer Jon Stewart. (Those were great, but they were too much work to make the transition onto the regular menu.) These newfangled pierogi have even made the return trip to Eastern Europe: Ala's daughter has a small restaurant in Warsaw where she sells pierogi, including some only-at-Veselka varieties.

As they work, the women place the completed pierogi on wooden pallets. A full pallet bears ten rows of four pierogi each, and it takes three and one-half pallets to fill a white bucket with pierogi.

The pierogi are then blanched until they float, which takes two to four minutes. When a customer places an order for pierogi, they are boiled a second time, topped with a dollop of sour cream and additional browned onion, and brought to the table piping hot and perfectly cooked. The resulting dish is stunningly good in its simplicity. Perhaps not all our customers fully appreciate the hard work of the pierogi team or are aware of the labor-intensive journey from kitchen to table, but they know a good thing when they taste it. Without pierogi, Veselka simply wouldn't be Veselka.

CHEESE BLINTZES

Makes 18 blintzes; about 9 servings

Blintzes are very similar to French crepes. In fact, if you own a well-seasoned crepe pan, use that here and don't oil it with cooking spray. Blintzes are usually filled with farmer's cheese and can be served plain or topped with sour cream, fruit, or a fruit sauce. They are an ideal brunch dish. We serve two blintzes to a serving at Veselka, but I bet you'll want at least three.

FILLING

2 pounds farmer's cheese

2 large eggs

½ cup sugar

¼ cup matzo meal

2 tablespoons vanilla extract

BATTER

1½ cups whole milk

15 large eggs

1½ cups durum (semolina) flour

½ cup cake flour

¾ cup vegetable oil

Vegetable oil cooking spray, for cooking the blintzes

1. In a medium bowl, combine all the ingredients for the filling. Mix with a fork and set aside.

2. To make the batter, in a large bowl combine the milk, eggs, flours, and oil with ½ cup cold water. Stir with a whisk until the batter is perfectly smooth. (A blender or an immersion blender is very useful for this.)

3. To make the blintzes, heat a medium cast-iron skillet or a griddle (or a well-seasoned crepe pan) over medium heat. When the pan is hot but not smoking, film it with a very small amount of vegetable oil cooking spray (except for the crepe pan, which shouldn't need any), being careful not to splatter yourself.

4. Ladle about ⅔ cup of the batter into the skillet and then tilt the pan in all directions to spread the batter thinly and evenly.

5. Cook over medium heat until the bottom is speckled with brown spots and the edges lift easily from the bottom of the pan, about 3 minutes. Adjust heat if the blintz is cooking too quickly or too slowly.

6. Use a spatula to flip the blintz and cook the other side for an additional 2 to 3 minutes.

7. Remove the blintz from the pan and set aside. Film the pan again and repeat with remaining batter.

8. When all the blintzes are cooked and have cooled, place one on the work surface with the more attractive side (probably the first side you cooked) facing down. Spread 3 to 4 tablespoons of the filling on one side of the blintz. Fold it down the center to form a semicircle. Repeat with remaining blintzes and filling. Blintzes can be made up to this point as much as one day in advance of serving.

9. When you are ready to serve the blintzes, melt about 1 tablespoon of the butter in a large sauté pan and heat as many blintzes as you can, without crowding the pan, until they are lightly browned on the bottom and the filling is heated through, 3 to 4 minutes, turning once. Serve immediately.

Variation: For Raspberry Blintzes, whisk together 3/4 cup sugar and 1/2 cup water in a small pot until the sugar has dissolved. Bring to a rolling boil, then turn off the heat and stir in 3 cups frozen raspberries and 1 teaspoon lemon juice. Refrigerate until chilled. Prepare the Cheese Blintzes exactly as above, then drizzle the raspberries over the folded blintzes and serve immediately.

MEAT-STUFFED CABBAGE

Makes 24 pieces; about 8 servings

Making stuffed cabbage—whether with this meat filling or the vegetarian mushroom and rice filling below—isn't difficult, but it's a multistep process. You can make the filling up to a couple days in advance, and the stuffed cabbage is actually better if it cools in the pot overnight in the refrigerator. And you may be pleasantly surprised to discover how pliable and easy to work with the cabbage leaves are when you use the freezing technique we use at the restaurant.

2 very large heads green cabbage	1 onion, diced
1 tablespoon salt	3½ pounds ground pork
3 tablespoons unsalted butter	1½ tablespoons freshly ground black pepper
3 cups short-grain white rice	2½ cups Chicken Stock (page 35)

1. At least one day before you want to make the stuffed cabbage, core the heads of cabbage. Place the cabbage in a large plastic freezer bag and freeze.

2. The next day, bring 2 cups water to a boil in a medium pot. Add the salt and 2 tablespoons butter. Slowly sprinkle in the rice, then stir once, cover with a tight-fitting lid, and simmer over low heat for 20 minutes, undisturbed. Check the rice and cook a little longer to absorb all the water, if necessary. When the rice is cooked, set it aside to cool.

3. Sauté the diced onion in the remaining 1 tablespoon butter, stirring occasionally, until they are a deep, rich brown, about 15 minutes. Set aside to cool.

4. In a large bowl, combine the cooked and cooled rice, the cooked and cooled onion, the pork, and the pepper. Gradually add the chicken stock in small amounts while mixing the mixture by hand. The mixture should be moist, but not soupy, and there should be no liquid in the bottom of the bowl. You may not need all the stock, or even any of it—this can vary.

5. When you are ready to stuff the cabbage, pull the cabbage out of the freezer. Fill a large bowl with warm water and place the cabbage in the water to defrost. When the leaves are pliable, peel them off the head one at a time and set them aside, being careful not to tear them. If a few do tear, reserve those for the bottom of the pot.

6. Place 3 or 4 leaves (including any torn ones) in the bottom of a very large pot. On top of the leaves place a heat-resistant plate or overturned pie pan or flat-bottomed steamer basket that sits about 1 inch above the bottom of the pot.

7. Place one cabbage leaf on the work surface. Place about ½ cup of stuffing in the center of the leaf and fold it envelope style (see illustration below) to enclose the filling. Turn the leaf over and place it seam-side down in the pot on top of the plate or pie pan or steamer basket. Repeat with remaining leaves and filling. As you fold each leaf, tuck it tightly up against the others in the pot in a single layer. They should be touching on all sides and wedged together very firmly. When you've made one layer of cabbage packets, continue with a second layer on top, and so on until you have used up all the leaves and filling. Depending on the size of your pot, you will probably have 4 or 5 layers of packets.

8. Add enough water to fill the pot about 5 inches up the side (some packets may be submerged—this is fine). Cover, and place over high heat for 1 to 2 minutes to build up some steam, then lower the heat and steam the cabbage until the leaves are tender and the pork mixture is cooked through, about 1½ hours. Keep an eye on the water in the bottom of the pot to be sure it doesn't dry out; add a little extra water as the cabbage cooks if necessary.

9. Allow the cabbage to cool in the pot, preferably overnight in the refrigerator, but at least for a couple of hours. This keeps the packets from unfurling when you remove them. Serve with either Tomato Sauce (page 55) or Mushroom Sauce (page 56).

Envelope Fold

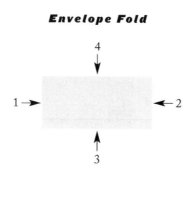

MUSHROOM-STUFFED CABBAGE

Makes 24 pieces; about 8 servings

Stuffed cabbage isn't a dish that you want to whip up at the last minute when unexpected guests drop in. However, it is a dish that freezes extraordinarily well, so you may want to make a big batch and freeze some in a foil tray. Then you can simply warm the cabbage in the oven until it is heated through and serve unexpected guests something delicious. If you're not crazy about the idea of using canned soup, you can substitute with additional stock, but your rice filling won't be as rich. That's how this dish is made for the meat- and dairy-free Christmas Eve meal (page 176); oil is used in place of the butter as well.

2 very large heads green cabbage

3 cups short-grain white rice

3 pounds button mushrooms

1 tablespoon vegetable oil

1 medium onion, diced

3 tablespoons unsalted butter

2 large eggs, lightly beaten

1 tablespoon freshly ground black pepper

One 10-ounce can cream of mushroom
  soup

½ to 1 cup Vegetable Stock (page 36)

1. At least one day before you want to make the stuffed cabbage, core the heads of cabbage. Place the cabbage in a large plastic freezer bag and freeze.
2. The next day bring 6 cups of water to a boil in a large stockpot. Stir in the rice. Cover, reduce the heat to medium, and simmer for 20 minutes or until all of the water is absorbed. Set aside to cool.
3. Clean and trim the mushrooms, then chop them very fine (a food processor fitted with the metal blade is ideal for doing this in batches). Sauté the mushrooms in the oil until the mushrooms are very soft and all of their liquid has released and evaporated, about 30 minutes.
4. In a large sauté pan, sauté the diced onion in the butter, stirring occasionally, until they are a deep, rich brown, about 15 minutes. Set aside to cool.
5. When you are ready to stuff the cabbage, pull the cabbage out of the freezer. Fill a large bowl with warm water and place the cabbage in the water to defrost.

When the leaves are pliable, peel them off the head and set aside, being careful not to tear them. If a few do tear, set those aside for the bottom of the pot.

6. In a large bowl combine the cooked and cooled rice, cooked and cooled mushrooms (if any liquid has collected, transfer them with a slotted spoon and discard the liquid), cooked and cooled onions, eggs, black pepper, and cream of mushroom soup. Stir with a spoon until thoroughly combined. If needed to reach the right consistency—moist but not soupy, and with no liquid in the bottom of the bowl, similar to the texture of ground beef—gradually add stock in small amounts.

7. Place 3 or 4 leaves (including any torn ones) in the bottom of a very large pot. On top of the leaves place a heat-resistant plate or overturned pie pan or flat-bottomed steamer basket that sits about 1 inch above the bottom of the pot.

8. Place one cabbage leaf on the work surface. Place about ½ cup of stuffing in the center of the leaf and fold it envelope style (see illustration on page 52) to enclose the filling. Turn the leaf over and place it seam-side down in the pot on top of the leaves. Repeat with remaining leaves and filling. As you fold each leaf, tuck it tightly up against the others in the pot in a single layer. They should be touching on all sides and wedged together very firmly. When you've made one layer of cabbage packets, continue with a second layer on top, and so on until you have used up all the leaves and filling. Depending on the size of your pot, you should have 4 or 5 layers of packets.

9. Add enough water to fill the pot about 5 inches (some packets may be submerged—this is fine). Cover, and place over high heat for 1 to 2 minutes to build up some steam, then lower the heat and steam the cabbage until the leaves are tender, about 1½ hours. Keep an eye on the water in the bottom of the pot to be sure it doesn't dry out; add a little extra water as the cabbage cooks if necessary.

10. Allow the cabbage to cool in the pot, preferably overnight in the refrigerator, but at least for a couple of hours. This keeps the packets from unfurling when you remove them. Serve with either Tomato Sauce (page 55) or Mushroom Sauce (page 56).

TOMATO SAUCE FOR STUFFED CABBAGE

Makes about 2 cups sauce; enough for 24 pieces

For years, there was the idea that tomato sauce had to simmer for hours in order to be properly cooked, but these days there are such high-quality canned tomatoes available that making tomato sauce is not a day-long project.

1 tablespoon olive oil

1 small onion, minced

1 garlic clove, minced

2½ cups canned tomato purée

Salt

1. In a medium pot, heat the olive oil over medium heat.
2. Add the onion and cook, stirring occasionally, until softened, about 3 minutes.
3. Add the garlic and cook until garlic is softened, about 2 minutes. Add the tomato purée and stir to combine. Cook at a gentle simmer until the liquid has evaporated and the sauce has thickened but is still pourable, about 10 minutes.
4. Season to taste with salt. Drizzle the sauce over the stuffed cabbage while hot.

MUSHROOM SAUCE FOR STUFFED CABBAGE

Makes about 2 cups sauce; enough for 24 pieces

At Veselka we roast huge amounts of mushrooms every day for stuffed cabbage, soup, and loads of other uses. Here's a simplified version of our mushroom sauce that you can make without turning on the oven to roast just a few mushrooms.

2 tablespoons unsalted butter

1 small onion, diced

8 ounces button mushrooms, stemmed,
  cleaned, and sliced

1 cup sour cream

2 tablespoons all-purpose flour

Salt

Freshly ground black pepper

1. Heat the butter in a large sauté pan. Add the onion and cook over medium heat, stirring occasionally, until translucent, about 5 minutes.
2. Add the mushrooms and continue cooking over medium heat until the mushrooms have given up their liquid and cooked down, about 10 minutes.
3. In a small bowl, whisk together the sour cream and flour.
4. Add the sour cream mixture to the mushrooms and cook, stirring constantly, until the liquid just begins to bubble.
5. Season to taste with salt and pepper, then reduce the heat until just an occasional bubble breaks the surface. Cover the pan and allow to simmer, undisturbed, for 5 minutes. Drizzle the sauce over stuffed cabbage while hot.

3
MEAT AND POULTRY

Ola's Famous Veal Goulash

Beef Stroganoff

   Chicken Stroganoff

Boiled Beef with Horseradish

   Sauce

Bigos (Pork Stew with Sauerkraut

   and Onions)

Grilled Ukrainian Kielbasa

Ukrainian Meatballs

Grilled Marinated Chicken Breasts

Boneless Breaded Chicken

   Cutlets

Chicken Pot Pie

BECAUSE MEAT WAS A LUXURY in the Ukraine, many of our more traditional Ukrainian meat and poultry dishes use meat as a condiment or one of several ingredients. It rarely appears in the form of a piece of meat in the center of the plate. The good news is that, nutritionally speaking, this is a healthier way to eat meat anyway.

And Ukrainian meat dishes are belly fillers. When you dig into a bowl of veal goulash or *bigos* (a stew of pork, sauerkraut, and onions) you won't go to bed hungry. Of course, at Veselka we have lots of other meat and poultry options, too. Our chicken breast marinated in rosemary and white wine is extremely popular. It's served with kasha or potatoes and a vegetable. It's just plain, good, satisfying food, and our technique for marinating the breast keeps it moist and tender. Our meatballs are made from a combination of pork and beef, so they're very moist as well. There are also plenty of main-course appropriate dishes in other places in this book. We have a whole chapter on sandwiches, and the stuffed cabbage and pierogi make excellent entrées. In fact, among the most-ordered items at Veselka is our meat combination plate, which includes soup, salad, stuffed cabbage, pierogi, and beet salad. It doesn't include a traditional entrée, but you'd be hard-pressed to say that that's not a meal.

We continue to purchase much of our meat from Julian Baczynsky, a Ukrainian butcher in our East Village neighborhood. (See page 247 for more about the store.) If you don't have a large Eastern European community where you live, see Resources on page 247 for places to order specialty meats such as kielbasa.

OLA'S FAMOUS VEAL GOULASH

Serves 6 to 8

Goulash, a meat stew, cleverly stretches a small amount of meat to serve many. Serve with Mashed Potatoes (page 99) or egg noodles.

4 pounds veal shoulder, cut into 1½-inch
  cubes

½ cup all-purpose flour

3 tablespoons olive oil

1 large onion, minced

2 cups Chicken Stock (page 35)

4 cups Vegetable Stock (page 36)

2 tablespoons ketchup

2 tablespoons Dijon mustard

1 teaspoon paprika

1 teaspoon freshly ground black pepper

4 whole allspice berries

3 bay leaves

1 tablespoon cornstarch

1. Dredge the meat in the flour. In a large sauté pan, heat the olive oil over medium heat. Working in batches if necessary, cook the meat in the olive oil until browned on all sides, about 5 minutes. Set aside.

2. In a medium stockpot, combine the onion, stocks, ketchup, mustard, paprika, pepper, allspice berries, and bay leaves. Bring to a boil, then lower to a simmer and add the browned meat. Using a ladle, transfer about ½ cup of broth from the stockpot to the pan used to brown the meat and deglaze the pan. Return the broth and any drippings and bits that you have scraped off of the pan to the pot with the rest of the broth.

3. Simmer gently, stirring occasionally, until the meat is tender, about 2 hours. Occasionally skim off any foam that rises to the top and discard it.

4. In a small bowl, dissolve the cornstarch in ¼ cup cold water. Add about 1 cup of the hot liquid from the pot to the cornstarch mixture and stir to combine, then return all of the cornstarch mixture to the pot.

5. Bring the goulash back to a boil and stir vigorously to make sure the cornstarch mixture is thoroughly combined. Then reduce the heat to low and simmer until the liquid has thickened, 15 to 20 minutes.

BEEF STROGANOFF

Serves 6 to 8

Like Veal Goulash, this is a belly filling meal-in-a-bowl, perfect for cold weather. Serve it with egg noodles or rice. Also like Ola's Veal Goulash, this recipe includes some ketchup. Interestingly, our Eastern European cooks don't see ketchup as a condiment—for them it's interchangeable with tomato paste, probably because they didn't have it on their tables when they were growing up. You can substitute tomato paste for the ketchup without any loss of flavor, though the resulting dish will taste slightly different than it does at Veselka.

5 pounds pepper steak strips	2 yellow onions, sliced (about 1½ cups)
1 cup all-purpose flour	4 large portobello mushrooms, sliced
2 tablespoons olive oil	8 ounces shiitake mushrooms, sliced
8 cups Chicken Stock (page 35)	8 ounces button mushrooms, sliced
4 tablespoons ketchup	2 cups sour cream
2 bay leaves	1 teaspoon cornstarch
4 whole allspice berries	Salt
8 tablespoons (1 stick) unsalted butter	Freshly ground black pepper

1. Rinse the meat and pat dry. Dredge the meat in the flour.
2. In a large cast-iron skillet, heat the olive oil and pan fry the meat until completely browned on all sides. (Cook in batches if necessary.)
3. Meanwhile, combine the chicken stock and ketchup in a large stockpot or Dutch oven and bring to a boil. Remove the cooked meat from the skillet with tongs or a slotted spoon (let any excess fat drip back into the skillet) and place the meat in the pot with the stock. (Pour off excess fat and set the skillet aside for step 5.) The stock should just cover the meat in the pot. If necessary, add a small amount of additional stock or some water.
4. Add the bay leaves and whole allspice berries to the pot. Simmer the beef until very tender, about 1½ hours, skimming occasionally.
5. In the same cast-iron skillet you used to cook the meat, melt the butter. Add the onions and cook over medium heat, stirring occasionally, until the onions are a

deep rich brown, about 11 minutes. Add the mushrooms and sauté until they are fully cooked, 10 to 15 additional minutes. Remove from heat and set aside.

6. When the meat is cooked, remove about 2 cups of cooking liquid from the pot and transfer to a medium bowl. Stir the sour cream into the hot liquid. Add the cornstarch to the sour cream and whisk vigorously to remove any lumps. This mixture should be very creamy and somewhat thick. Return the sour cream mixture to the pot, stir to combine with the meat, and bring to a boil. Reduce the heat to low and simmer until thickened, about 10 minutes.

7. Stir in the mushrooms and onions and season to taste with salt and pepper. Serve hot.

Variations: To make Chicken Stroganoff, replace the pepper steak with boneless, skinless chicken breasts cut into strips and decrease the stock to 2^1/2 cups. In step 4, simmer the chicken for only 15 to 20 minutes, and in step 6, stir only 1 cup of cooking liquid into the sour cream. Omit the ketchup or reduce to 2 tablespoons.

BOILED BEEF WITH HORSERADISH SAUCE

Serves 6 to 8

This isn't on our regular menu, but it is a frequent special. While boiled beef may not sound particularly interesting, this is actually a very flavorful dish. The brisket gets very tender cooked this way, and the sauce has a wonderful bite.

One 5-pound brisket, trimmed	3 carrots, peeled and roughly chopped
1 teaspoon ground allspice	1 onion, peeled and halved
Salt	½ cup sour cream
Freshly ground black pepper	½ cup buttermilk
3 celery stalks, roughly chopped	3 tablespoons prepared horseradish

1. Place the brisket in a Dutch oven or other large pot. Add the allspice and water just to cover the brisket. Season to taste with salt and pepper.

2. Bring to a boil, then skim any foam from the top. Reduce to a simmer, and add the celery, carrots, and onion, and simmer until the brisket is very tender and can be pulled apart with a fork, 2 to 3 hours.

3. While the brisket is cooking, make the horseradish sauce. Whisk together the sour cream, buttermilk, and 1 tablespoon of the horseradish. Taste and adjust the amount of horseradish. Season to taste with salt and pepper.

4. When the brisket is cooked, remove it from the broth to a platter and slice into ¼-inch slices. With a slotted spoon, remove the vegetables from the broth and transfer them to the platter. Moisten the meat with a little broth just before serving. (Any leftover broth can be degreased and eaten as a soup course or frozen for later use.) Serve the meat and vegetables on the platter with the sauce on the side. If the sauce has separated a little, whisk again just before serving.

BIGOS

(PORK STEW WITH SAUERKRAUT AND ONIONS)

Serves 4 to 6

Bigos *is eaten in Ukraine and throughout Eastern Europe, but it is probably Poland's most famous dish. Many of the people who work in Veselka's kitchen are Polish (when I first came to Veselka, Ukrainians couldn't get out from behind the Soviet Union's iron curtain, so Ukrainian immigration to the United States was almost nil), and they brought this hearty stew to our menu. The word* bigos *means "big mess" in Polish, and presumably refers to the fact that this stew contains a little bit of everything. Bigos is good when it is first made, but I find it improves and intensifies with reheating. A slice of dark rye bread is perfect for soaking up the juices.*

4 cups Chicken Stock (page 35)

3 tablespoons olive oil

3 pounds boneless pork roast, cut into cubes

1 large onion, diced

6 whole allspice berries

1 teaspoon paprika

2 bay leaves

3 links kielbasa smoked sausage, thinly sliced

4 cups sauerkraut with juices

Freshly ground black pepper

1. In a medium pot, combine the stock with 1½ cups water and bring to a boil. Reduce to a simmer and keep warm until you are ready to use it. Preheat the oven to 400°F.

2. Meanwhile, heat the oil in a large pot over medium heat, and add the pork. Working in batches, if necessary, cook, turning with tongs, until the pieces are browned on all sides, about 5 minutes.

3. Pour the hot stock mixture over the meat. Add the diced onion, allspice, paprika, and bay leaves. Simmer until the meat is very tender, about 1½ hours.

4. Place the kielbasa links in a single layer in a roasting pan and roast in the preheated oven, turning once, until they are browned and a little crispy, 20 to 25 minutes. Remove and set aside.

5. While the pork is cooking, prepare the sauerkraut: Place the sauerkraut in a medium pot with its juices. Bring to a boil and cook for 5 minutes. Drain the sauerkraut, but do not rinse it. Set aside.

6. When the pork is fully cooked and very tender, stir in the cooked kielbasa and the blanched sauerkraut. Simmer for 10 minutes to combine the flavors. Season to taste with pepper and serve hot.

GRILLED UKRAINIAN KIELBASA

Serves 8

We get delicious, meaty kielbasa from our long-time butcher, Julian Baczynsky. It consists mainly of pork, but also includes some beef, and it is very lightly smoked. Preparing it couldn't be any more simple—serve with plenty of mustard and sauerkraut. (See Resources on page 247 for more information on purchasing kielbasa.)

2 pounds kielbasa smoked sausage

1. Prepare a grill for cooking.
2. If necessary, cut the kielbasa in half in order to fit it onto your grill. Slice the kielbasa lengthwise. With a sharp knife, cut crosshatch marks into the skin sides of the sausage.
3. Grill the kielbasa on the grill rack, turning once, until charred with grill marks and heated through, about 2 minutes per side. Serve hot.

Baczynsky the Butcher

When I began working at Veselka in the late 1960s, there was a Ukrainian man renovating a store right across Second Avenue. I'd talk to him occasionally about the work he was doing, and then in 1970 the store opened. That man was Julian Baczynsky and the store was East Village Meat Market (known to everyone as Baczynsky's, no matter what it says on the sign), and I had no idea what a big presence he'd be in my life.

At that time, there were several Ukrainian butcher shops scattered around the East Village, and numerous Polish ones, too, which sold very similar things—homemade kielbasa, baloney, ham, as well as fresh cuts of all kinds of meat. Like many immigrants, when Ukrainians came to the United States, they found themselves able to afford to eat meat—back home a treat reserved for holidays and Sundays—almost daily.

Mr. Baczynsky (even now it's hard for me to call him anything but that) had owned two butcher shops in the area with a partner, but the partner's son came into the business with his father, so Baczynsky struck out on his own.

The East Village Meat Market is located conveniently across the street from Veselka. *(Ben Fink)*

Butcher Julian Baczynsky has supplied kielbasa and other meat to Veselka since 1970. *(Ben Fink)*

Being across the street from Veselka was great advertising, he recalls, "Everybody knows about Veselka. Who didn't know Mr. Darmochwal? Everybody knew him—doctors, professors, everybody."

Today, Baczynsky is the last man standing. The other Eastern European butchers in the area may have gone out of business, but at eighty-six, Baczynsky is going strong. He can still be found in the store every day, though he has two men who run things for him now. When I see him there, constantly checking on the quality of his meat, readjusting items in the showcase, and bantering with customers, I'm reminded of what Veselka's founder, Wolodymyr Darmochwal, used to say to workers he didn't think were pulling their weight: "If you want to stand with your arms folded, get a job at a museum."

Baczynsky represents the classic immigrant success story, and it's all been achieved through hard work. Though he had earned a degree in forestry engineering, when he came to the United States in 1949 as a twenty-five-year-old, his first job was washing dishes in a restaurant for four dollars a day.

Today, Veselka is his biggest customer: We buy about two hundred pounds of his smoked pork-and-beef kielbasa sausage weekly, and Baczynsky makes a specially sized link just for the restaurant. New York state agricultural officials dealt a big blow to Eastern European butchers a few years ago when they deemed that kielbasa—which is smoked and therefore preserved—could no longer hang in the open air on hooks. Baczynsky still gets worked up when he recalls the inspectors coming to his store. He says, "I told the inspector, 'Look, I make kielbasa fifty years, and nobody was ever sick from my kielbasa. You don't know what is the kielbasa. When you hang kielbasa to dry it, the water goes out and it's more tasty.' I was so mad. I'm still mad."

Despite those changes, Baczynsky does a brisk business. He ships his products far and wide, but only in the winter months (see Resources on page 247 for details), and he gets a big kick out of telling you about people who come from all over to buy meat from his store. Indeed, at Easter time, cars with license plates from New Jersey, Pennsylvania, and even farther park outside his store on Second Avenue, and a long line of customers wait to pick up hams. (Baczynsky makes five different kinds of ham, and I find they all have a unique flavor, maybe due to the maple wood used to smoke them.)

Baczynsky gleefully reports that a customer once flew in on a private plane from Nicaragua to buy kielbasa. And our butcher even makes special deliveries on occasion: His eyes twinkle as he tells me that now that so many of his generation have passed away, "I go to cemetery to visit. I take two shopping bags of kielbasa and put one on each grave." His own father lived to be ninety years old and sometimes lent a hand in the store as well.

Baczynsky hasn't been back to Ukraine since he left in 1949, but for the last fourteen years, he and his wife of sixty-plus years have generously funded an orphanage in that country that houses 125 children. They send clothing, food, and money, and Baczynsky works tirelessly to collect funds from me and other local businesspeople and residents. He's very proud of this endeavor, and equally proud that he gets low prices on the items he sends over. His secret? "I buy at Kmart when it's on clearance," he tells me, "and there's a Polish lady who's a manager over there. I bring her kielbasa and she gives me a discount."

UKRAINIAN MEATBALLS

Makes fifteen 4-ounce meatballs; about 6 servings

These delicious meatballs may be either baked or fried. Pan-frying gives them a crunchy exterior, while baking leaves them slightly softer. Either way, they are delicious.

1 large stale sandwich roll, such as a Kaiser roll, torn into pieces

1 cup whole milk

2½ pounds ground pork or beef or a combination of the two

2 large eggs, lightly beaten

1 small yellow onion, minced

2 garlic cloves, minced

2 teaspoons salt

1 tablespoon freshly ground black pepper

1 cup dry bread crumbs

1 tablespoon olive oil

1. If you are planning to bake the meatballs, preheat the oven to 375°F. If you prefer your meatballs with a crispy crust, bake at a higher temperature for a shorter period of time.

2. Soak the bread in the milk until soft, about 10 minutes.

3. In a large bowl, combine the meat, eggs, onion, garlic, salt, and pepper. Remove the soaked bread from the milk and pinch it into small pieces right into the bowl with the meat. Mix with your hands until well combined.

4. Roll the meat mixture into 15 round or oval meatballs.

5. Spread the bread crumbs on a large plate and roll the meatballs in them to coat the outsides.

6. To bake the meatballs, place them on a jelly-roll pan, drizzle them with olive oil, and bake in the preheated oven, turning them a few times, until browned, about 30 minutes.

7. To pan-fry the meatballs, heat the 1 tablespoon olive oil in a large sauté pan. Cook the meatballs in the pan, turning them with tongs to brown on all sides. Cook in batches if necessary to avoid crowding the skillet.

GRILLED MARINATED CHICKEN BREASTS

Serves 4

The white meat of chicken is nutritionally sound and a great canvas that takes on any fla-vorings you throw at it. The only problem with chicken breasts is that they can be a bit dry, especially when they are grilled. Marinating is a simple solution to that problem. While this is the recipe we use at Veselka, you could play around with it in a lot of different ways, by adjusting the proportions of the seasonings or even adding different herbs, citrus or other fruit juices, or almost anything else you like.

2 cups dry white wine

¼ cup extra-virgin olive oil

2 tablespoons dried thyme

2 cloves garlic, minced

½ teaspoon salt

2 teaspoons freshly ground black pepper

4 boneless, skinless chicken breasts

1. In a medium glass dish large enough to hold the chicken breasts in a single layer, combine the wine, olive oil, thyme, garlic, salt, and pepper.

2. Place the chicken breasts in the marinade, turning a couple times to moisten both sides. Cover and refrigerate for at least 1 hour, or as long as overnight.

3. When you're ready to cook the chicken breasts, preheat a charcoal or gas grill or a broiler. Remove the breasts from the marinade; reserve the marinade.

4. Cook the breasts on a grill or under a broiler, basting a couple times with the reserved marinade, until cooked through, 5 to 10 minutes per side.

BONELESS BREADED CHICKEN CUTLETS

Serves 4

Panko, or Japanese-style bread crumbs, make the crispiest chicken cutlets there are. These cutlets are terrific on their own with a green salad and some rice, but they also make fabulous sandwiches.

4 large eggs

2 tablespoons lemon juice

1 tablespoon paprika

2 teaspoons freshly ground black pepper

¼ teaspoon salt

1 cup panko

3 tablespoons vegetable oil

4 boneless, skinless chicken breasts,
  pounded thin

1. In a medium bowl, whisk together the eggs, lemon juice, paprika, pepper, and salt.
2. Arrange the panko on a large plate.
3. Add the oil to a large cast-iron skillet or sauté pan and heat over medium heat for a few minutes.
4. When the oil is hot, dredge the pounded chicken breasts first in the egg mixture, then in the panko and place in the heated oil. Repeat with remaining chicken breasts. (You may need to cook them in batches if the skillet isn't large enough to hold all the breasts in one layer. If you do, add a little extra oil between batches and heat the oil again for a minute or so before adding the chicken breast.)
5. Cook the chicken until golden brown and cooked through, about 5 minutes on each side. Serve hot.

CHICKEN POT PIE

Serves 6 to 8

This recipe may be off-putting at first because of its length, but after you follow it one time you'll see the logic to it. Just read through the recipe once to be sure that you have the equipment you need and leave yourself time. You can prepare the chicken filling up to a day in advance, but the crust shouldn't sit too long or it may get soggy. If you don't have roasted garlic for the crust you can leave it out, but it does make this especially good, and it's simple as can be: Just peel the garlic cloves, toss them with a little olive oil, place on a small pan or baking dish, and put in a 350°F or 375°F oven until soft, 15 to 20 minutes. (The toaster oven is perfect for this, or you can do it when you have the oven on for another purpose.) If you want to roast a whole head of garlic, remove the papery outer skin, but leave the cloves attached with the harder inner skin still on. Roasted garlic will keep in the refrigerator in a jar for a couple of weeks.

FILLING

3 cups Chicken Stock (page 35)

2¼ pounds chicken parts (breasts, legs and thighs)

1 large carrot, peeled and diced

1 large Idaho potato, peeled and diced

1 celery stalk, peeled and diced

4 ounces button mushrooms, stemmed and quartered

¾ cup frozen peas

2 tablespoons unsalted butter

1 small onion, chopped

2 tablespoons all-purpose flour

¼ cup plus 2 tablespoons heavy cream

½ teaspoon salt

½ teaspoon freshly ground black pepper

1 teaspoon chopped fresh oregano, or more to taste

2 teaspoons chopped fresh parsley, or more to taste

CRUST

1½ cups all-purpose flour

1 teaspoon salt

1 tablespoon baking powder

2 teaspoons sugar

1 teaspoon freshly ground black pepper

½ teaspoon dried oregano

2 roasted garlic cloves, smashed with a fork

1¼ cups heavy cream

1. For the filling, place the chicken stock and chicken parts in a large pot or Dutch oven, bring to a boil, skim off any foam, then turn down the heat and simmer until the chicken is cooked through, about 1 hour.

2. Remove the cooked chicken and set aside to cool. Skim the stock again. Return the stock to a simmer and add the carrots. Simmer the carrots and potato for 5 minutes, then add the celery. Simmer for 5 additional minutes, then add the mushrooms and peas. Simmer for 5 additional minutes, then remove the cooked vegetables with a slotted spoon and set aside, but leave the stock at a gentle simmer.

3. Melt 1 tablespoon of the butter in a large sauté pan. Add the onion and sauté until translucent, about 5 minutes. Remove onion with a slotted spoon and add to the other cooked vegetables, but return the pan to stove.

4. Skim the stock once more. In the sauté pan, melt the remaining 1 tablespoon butter, then add the flour. Cook over medium heat for 5 minutes, stirring constantly with a wooden spoon. The flour should start to brown slightly.

5. Whisk about 1 cup of hot stock from the pot into the flour mixture. When there are no lumps, add as much stock as you can fit in the pan. Whisk until there are no lumps, then return the flour mixture to the pot with the stock. Whisk until there are no lumps. Cook this mixture in the pot, stirring frequently, until it no longer tastes of raw flour, about 30 minutes.

6. Meanwhile, preheat the oven to 350°F.

7. While the sauce is cooking, pull the chicken meat (which should now be cool enough to handle) from the bones, shredding it into large pieces with your fingers directly into a 2½-quart casserole dish. (A 13×9-inch baking dish will also work.) Add the cooked vegetables to the dish as well.

8. To make the crust, combine the flour, salt, baking powder, sugar, pepper, and oregano in a medium bowl. Stir with a fork to combine. Add the garlic and cream and mix with a fork until the dough forms a shaggy ball. Transfer the dough to a lightly floured work surface and knead 3 or 4 times just until it holds together, then roll out to ¾-inch thickness and to a size and shape that will fit on top of the casserole dish you are using.

9. Carefully transfer the prepared crust to a parchment-lined cookie sheet or jelly-roll pan and bake in the preheated oven until dry to the touch but not completely browned, about 12 minutes. (Leave the oven on.)

10. When the sauce is cooked, stir in the heavy cream, and strain the mixture through a fine-mesh strainer over the chicken in the casserole dish. Season the chicken and vegetable mixture with the salt and pepper and sprinkle with the oregano and parsley. Stir a couple times to combine everything and coat all the vegetables and chicken with sauce.

11. Using two spatulas, transfer the baked crust to the top of the casserole. (If the crust has not cooled completely it may crack a little, but don't sweat it—it's in keeping with the rustic quality of this dish. Just patch the crust together over the chicken mixture.) Bake the entire dish until the filling is heated through and the crust is golden brown, 10 to 15 minutes. Serve piping hot.

4

SALADS AND SIDE DISHES

East Village Spinach Salad with
   Creamy Dill Dressing

Roasted Beet and Goat Cheese
   Salad

Chef's Salad

Beet Salad

Lentil Salad

Vegetable Pâté

Coleslaw

Sauerkraut

Chicken Salad

Tuna Salad

Turkey Salad

Egg Salad

Potato Salad

Mashed Potatoes

Potato Pancakes

Home Fried Potatoes

Kasha

Macaroni and Cheese

SALADS AT VESELKA are more than a bowl full of greens—we pride ourselves on our Lentil Salad, Beet Salad with horseradish, and white meat Turkey Salad. Our Chef's Salad and other meals-in-a-bowl, when paired with a couple of slices of our Whole Wheat Bread (page 187), make a terrific balanced meal, especially in the summer, when you don't feel like heating up your kitchen. These salads offer an easy solution to doing what many nutritionists recommend these days—getting vegetables into the center of the plate, with a little meat or other protein served on the side.

My employees who go back and forth between the United States and Ukraine tell me that eating habits in their country of origin have changed tremendously in recent years, and the biggest change is that Ukrainians have vastly increased their consumption of vegetables. At Veselka, I try to incorporate more and more salads on the menu—who isn't trying to eat healthier these days?—but I do so with an eye to using Eastern European ingredients. For example, in the summer we often offer a platter of fruit salad and farmer's cheese, sort of a Ukrainian-style take on the old coffee shop "diet plate" of cottage cheese and pineapple. Our Beet Salad is very popular and offers an opportunity to use some of the cooked beets that we use to make the gallons of "beet water" that goes into Veselka's Famous Borscht (page 12). Recently I went to a very fancy restaurant with my wife, and she ordered "beet- and horseradish-crusted salmon." It came to the table and I tasted it, and it was delicious, but also very familiar. And then I realized it was a piece of perfectly grilled salmon with a Veselka-style beet salad resting on top of it.

When Wolodymyr Darmochwal added tuna salad and egg salad to the menu in the 1960s, he insisted on using Hellmann's mayonnaise in them, and I insist on the same thing today, even though it's pricier than most brands. Back then, a woman named Rosie came in and made just tuna salad and egg salad and a very basic vinaigrette salad dressing.

In keeping with our focus on good ingredients prepared simply, we don't use frozen vegetables as a side dish at Veselka. Instead, we steam broccoli, cauliflower, and carrots in big batches and serve those.

Our mashed potatoes are real, too, never made with powder or mix, and they're just one of several potato options on the menu. Ukrainians love potatoes almost as much as they love cabbage, and we serve them mashed, in home fries, or in potato pancakes. We also offer kasha—a kind of buckwheat pilaf—which makes a great change from rice or noodles when served alongside a stew or other entrée.

Artists of All Kinds

As I wrote in the introduction to this book, I consider myself an adopted member of New York's Ukrainian community, but there's another community in New York City that has adopted me (and Veselka): artists of all kinds.

In the late 1970s and especially the 1980s, the East Village went from being a sleepy Ukrainian neighborhood full of hard-working, first-generation immigrants to a lively, funky spot filled with bars and galleries and performance spaces. This kind of transformation happens frequently in New York City: A neighborhood where the real estate is relatively cheap fills up with artists, young people, and other interesting folk who don't have a lot of money.

When Wolodymyr Darmochwal, the founder of Veselka, was still alive, Veselka catered to an almost 100 percent Ukrainian clientele, but by the 1980s I'd opened up the restaurant, both literally and metaphorically. The dining area was much bigger, and it no longer operated like a private club, behind those blue velvet drapes. The artists and musicians who flooded into the area to live

This is a picture of the small core staff at Veselka, and myself, at the head of the table, in 1978 or 1979. The photo was taken in the old backroom, with the heavy blue drapes behind us. (*Author's Collection*)

here discovered Veselka very quickly. For me, one of the great satisfactions of running Veselka is getting to know so many creative people, and even sometimes to play a small part in their art.

The East Village wasn't famous for pretty, staid art, either. This was the home of seminal punk club CBGB (opened in 1973 and closed in 2006), ground zero for bands like The Ramones and The New York Dolls. Lenny Kaye, who played guitar for Patti Smith, once wrote a rap ode to Veselka on a napkin—today it's one of my most prized possessions. I also get a huge kick out of the song "Veselka" by Greta Gertler and the Extroverts on their 2008 CD *Edible Restaurant*, which opens with the lines, "There's a diner / down on 9th Street" and is all about Veselka. The recorded version of the song ends with ambient noise recorded in the restaurant. When the band performed at a club in the East Village and debuted the song, we provided pierogi for the audience afterward.

The multidisciplinary performance space PS122 opened on First Avenue and 9th Street in the 1980s and quickly became the center of the burgeoning genre of performance art. It is still going strong today. Mark Russell worked at PS122 at the time and says, "Veselka has been the canteen for PS122 since the beginning. At one time I was such a regular that the waitress would just bring over my bowl of borscht and cup of coffee immediately once I sat down. If I wanted something else, well, forget it, I could not change my order. Before cell phones the phone booths at Veselka were a crucial asset for chasing apartments or getting calls away from home, later checking your service to see if you had a job, or a date, or could go back to nursing your coffee and talking gossip with the other East Village artist refugees."

Dona McAdams, who became house photographer for PS122 in the early 1980s, remembers, "Most of the artists and performers I worked with used Veselka as an informal office and cafeteria. It was the hub. You could always find certain working artists at regular times of day. Mark Russell had his usual

window spot. Holly Hughes was often eating a bowl of oatmeal at the counter in the mornings. Kim Jones was at his corner table by the window with the *New York Times*. The Five Lesbian Brothers sat together in the back and a lot of the WOW Café hung out there—just to name a few. Tim Miller and John Bernd were counter guys. We all used the bank of old phones in the back to make

In the 1980s, the row of phone booths at the rear of Veselka served as an informal "office" for the many performance artists in the neighborhood. *(Mykola Darmochwal)*

PENNY ARCADE

BITCH!
DYKE!
FAGHAG!

WHORE

July 23rd through

August 23rd, 1992   9:00 PM Showtime $10.00

P.S. 122 150 First Avenue & Ninth Street Reservations: 212-477-5288

WHAM benefit August 1st 11:00 PM special show

This show is dedicated to Cookie Mueller and women everywhere. Care Aids Now ! End Censorship Now !

Performance artist Penny Arcade was such a loyal customer that we were sponsors of her show in 1992. She included an essay on the back of the program in which she lauded Veselka as a place with "Great food still cheap."

our appointments—they were oak I believe, and had important numbers carved into the wood. The little room in the back (under the loft) was where you'd go if you wanted to have a private talk or meeting. Pierogi were required in the winter. Cold borscht in the summer. It was comfort food that filled you up for little money."

La MaMa E.T.C. on 4th Street, opened by local hero Ellen Stewart in 1961, was also the site of a great deal of groundbreaking performance art. Performance artist Penny Arcade, a key player in that movement, perhaps best known for her one-woman show "BITCH!DYKE!FAGHAG!WHORE!," dates her first time as a Veselka customer back to 1967.

In 1990, four performance artists—John Fleck, Holly Hughes, Tim Miller, and Karen Finley—gained fame as the "NEA Four," when ultraconservative senator Jesse Helms got wind of the content of their work and demanded that the National Endowment for the Arts revoke their grants. (They sued the NEA and later won.) The three who lived in New York were longtime and loyal Veselka customers. (Fleck was based in Los Angeles.) Miller recalls that he ate breakfast at Veselka almost every day from 1979 to 1984. ("Everyone ate there," he says today.) Finley was known for dousing herself in foodstuffs, and when she staged a show in which she poured honey over her head in a golden stream, Veselka donated gallons of honey and received credit in the show's program. I've always felt proud of the part I played in their art—I like to imagine these avant-garde artists conceptualizing their work over bottomless cups of coffee and bowls of borscht.

In addition to feeding the dramatic community here, Veselka has hosted it as a kind of living stage set. In 2008, a short play titled *Etiquette* that was part of the Under the Radar Festival took place at a table in the restaurant as a site-specific project. At each performance, two volunteers donned headphones through which they received orders as to what to say and do—instructions included drawing on their own skin and clapping loudly.

Veselka even has its own "artist-in-residence," painter Arnie Charnick, who has held that title since 1982. Arnie is responsible for both the mural on the outside of the restaurant and the monochromatic diner mural on the inside that is being dismantled and sold, as we're about to knock down that wall. And a group of Veselka's less famous customers got into the art game in 1992, when they worked with us to develop a new menu design, with the now-familiar coffee cup logo, which won second place in the National Restaurant Association's Great Menu Contest.

Veselka has served as set or back-drop in a lot of movies, too, most recently *Nick and Norah's Infinite Playlist*, about a young couple's odyssey around New York City at night. The well-known director Bart Freundlich has frequented Veselka since he was a student at NYU Film School. In fact, he filmed his student thesis here, with my permission. These days Freundlich often drops by in the company of his wife, actress Juli-

Customers helped us design an award-winning menu in 1992, including Veselka's now-familiar coffee cup logo. *(Ben Fink)*

anne Moore. Indeed, a large number of actors and actresses from film and theater as well as musicians in all genres fill the seats at Veselka. Jon Voight—who fueled himself with our pierogi when he was young and poor and living in the East Village—loves Veselka, and so do indie favorites Parker Posey and Steve Buscemi. Actress Chloe Sevigny often drops in for breakfast, but never before two o'clock in the afternoon. And before Jon Stewart became famous as host of *The Daily Show* on Comedy Central, we knew him as that nice struggling comedian who loved our pierogi.

But while Veselka is a celebrity hangout, it's not a flashy place where paparazzi stalk their prey—not Elaine's or the Waverly Inn. Instead, Veselka is the type of place where you're likely to be sitting at the counter, enjoying a piece of apple crumb cake, when you turn to your left and realize Lou Reed is perched on the next stool over, munching a fried egg sandwich. Indeed, Veselka's humble atmosphere works a kind of magic: Stars don't act like primadonnas here, and in return, nobody bothers them. Smashing Pumpkins guitarist James Iha sat at the counter every day for years before a new short-order cook who was a fan recognized him. "Are you . . . ?" he asked. Iha nodded and went right back to his blintzes.

EAST VILLAGE SPINACH SALAD WITH CREAMY DILL DRESSING

Serves 4

Spinach is a nutritional powerhouse and even better for you when served raw. The key to a delicious spinach salad is locating tender, young spinach. If all you can get your hands on are the tougher, more fibrous leaves, steam them instead. They will just never make a truly tasty salad. At the restaurant, we offer the option of topping this salad with some sliced Grilled Marinated Chicken Breasts (page 71), which rounds it out into a full meal.

DRESSING

¼ cup plain yogurt

¼ cup sour cream

1 tablespoon lemon juice

½ teaspoon salt

¼ teaspoon freshly ground black pepper

2 tablespoons chopped fresh dill

1 to 2 tablespoons whole milk, if needed

SALAD

4 strips bacon

12 button mushrooms (one 8-ounce package)

1 pound baby spinach

2 large carrots, peeled and thinly sliced

2 hard-boiled eggs, peeled and sliced

1. To make the dressing, whisk together all the ingredients in a small bowl. The dressing can be made in advance and even benefits from a day in the refrigerator. The thickness of the dressing varies depending on the yogurt and sour cream—if it seems too thick, thin with a little milk.

2. To make the salad, cook the bacon over medium heat in a cast-iron pan until very crispy, about 10 minutes. Set aside on paper towels to blot and cool.

3. Meanwhile, remove and discard the stems from the mushrooms. Clean with a brush or damp paper towels and slice the caps about ⅛ inch thick.

4. Clean the spinach in several changes of cold water until the water runs clear. Tear off and discard any spinach stems. If the leaves are large, tear them in half.

5. To assemble the salad, place the spinach in a salad bowl. Crumble the cooled bacon on top. Add the sliced mushrooms, sliced carrots, and sliced egg. Either top with the dressing and toss to combine, or serve the dressing on the side.

ROASTED BEET AND GOAT CHEESE SALAD

Serves 4

The combination of salty goat cheese, sweet oranges and candied nuts, and earthy beets is a sure-fire winner. My friend Angela Miller is not only a literary agent, but also a goat cheesemaker. If you can find her stellar Bardwell Farms goat cheese, I highly recommend using it.

4 to 6 small beets

⅔ cup plus 1 tablespoon extra-virgin olive
  oil

1 cup walnut halves

½ cup light corn syrup

¼ cup sugar

6 cups mesclun

4 ounces goat cheese

One 14-ounce can mandarin orange
  segments in water, drained

⅓ cup balsamic vinegar

Salt to taste

Freshly ground black pepper to taste

1. To roast beets, preheat oven to 375°F. Trim beets, but do not peel. Place beets on a large square of aluminum foil, drizzle with 1 tablespoon of the oil, and roast until tender, 30 minutes to 1 hour. Cool, peel, dice, and set aside. Beets may be prepared 2 days in advance and refrigerated.

2. To make candied walnuts, preheat oven to 325°F (or use a toaster oven). Toss the walnuts with the corn syrup and sugar and spread in one layer on a sheet pan. Toast until nuts turn darker and syrup thickens, being careful not to burn them, about 20 minutes. Cool and break apart. Nuts may be prepared 2 days in advance and stored in an airtight container.

3. Divide the mesclun among 4 individual salad bowls. Divide diced beets in the center of each dish, and top with a portion of goat cheese and orange slices. Sprinkle on walnuts. In a small bowl, combine remaining ⅔ cup oil, vinegar, and salt and pepper to taste. Whisk to emulsify and moisten each salad with a little dressing, passing the rest on the side.

CHEF'S SALAD

Serves 4

A chef's salad with turkey, ham, hard-boiled egg, and cheese makes a great warm-weather dinner. Add a nice loaf of bread and some sliced berries for dessert, and you've got a feast. I like a chef's salad best with vinaigrette—there's so much going on that I find a creamy dressing or one with strong flavors a bit of overkill—but if your preferences run in another direction, feel free to substitute your favorite. Also, if you find cherry or grape tomatoes that look better than salad tomatoes, use those instead. The turkey, ham, and cheese strips should all be more or less the same size, about ¼ inch wide and 2 inches long. Don't use processed meats in this salad—go for real roasted turkey breast and good baked ham. You'll taste the difference.

DRESSING

½ cup extra-virgin olive oil

3 tablespoons red wine vinegar

½ teaspoon salt

¼ teaspoon freshly ground black pepper

SALAD

1 head romaine lettuce

1 pound mesclun

2 tomatoes, sliced

2 cucumbers, peeled and sliced into thin
　　rounds

2 red bell peppers, seeded and cut into cut
　　into thin strips

1 cup homemade (or best-quality,
　　store-bought) roasted turkey breast, cut
　　into strips

1 cup best-quality baked ham, cut into
　　strips

1 cup cheddar, Muenster, Swiss, or
　　American cheese (or a combination of
　　two or more), cut into strips

4 hard-boiled eggs, peeled and sliced

1. To make the dressing, combine all the ingredients in a small bowl and whisk until combined. Set aside.
2. To make the salad, tear off and discard any wilted leaves around the outside of the head of romaine. Tear off the leaves and discard the hard, white core. Wash the romaine leaves in several changes of cold water and line a platter or large salad bowl with the leaves.
3. Wash the mesclun in several changes of cold water. In a separate large bowl, toss together the mesclun (torn into small pieces if the leaves are large) with the tomato, cucumber, and bell pepper.
4. Give the dressing another quick whisk and toss the mesclun mixture with about half of the dressing. Mound the mesclun mixture on top of the romaine.
5. Sprinkle the turkey, ham, cheese, and hard-boiled egg over the mesclun mixture. Drizzle on the remaining dressing or serve the remaining dressing on the side.

BEET SALAD

Serves 4

This is a great way to use up the cooked beets you have left after making "beet water" for any of the borscht recipes in this book. If you don't have any cooked beets on hand, you can either peel and chop beets and steam them, or, even easier, wrap them in aluminum foil, roast them in a 350°F oven until they are tender (45 minutes to 1 hour—try and do this in a toaster oven or when the oven is on for another purpose), then slip off the skins and mince them. I'm providing measurements here, but obviously, you can make as much or as little as you like, and the amount of horseradish here is just a guideline—if you like enough horseradish to make your eyes tear, add more.

2 cups cooked chopped beets

2 tablespoons prepared horseradish

Salt, if needed

1. Place the cooked beets in a medium bowl. Add about 1 tablespoon of the horseradish to start and stir to combine. Taste and add more horseradish, if desired.

2. Taste again and season to taste with salt (depending on how strong your horseradish is, you may not feel you need any). Serve cold or at room temperature.

LENTIL SALAD

Serves 4

Lentils are the fastest cooking legumes, plus they taste great and are very healthy. You don't need to wait for the lentils to cool in step 1 before proceeding with the recipe—in fact, the lentils will meld better with the other ingredients if you don't.

¾ cup green lentils

3 tablespoons olive oil

2 garlic cloves, minced

1 celery stalk, minced

1 red bell pepper, seeded and minced

1 small carrot, peeled and minced

1 tablespoon balsamic vinegar

1 tablespoon chopped fresh flat-leaf parsley

½ teaspoon freshly ground black pepper

½ teaspoon salt

½ pound mesclun

¼ cup crumbled feta

1. Place the lentils in a large stockpot with abundant water to cover. Bring to a boil, then reduce the heat to low and simmer until the lentils are tender, about 30 minutes. Drain and set aside in a large bowl.

2. In a small sauté pan, heat the olive oil. Sauté the garlic, celery, red pepper, and carrot until softened, about 5 minutes.

3. Stir the cooked vegetable mixture into the lentils. Add the vinegar, parsley, pepper, and salt and stir to combine. Refrigerate for at least 1 hour and as long as 2 days.

4. To serve the salad, spread the mesclun leaves on a serving platter. Taste the lentil mixture and adjust seasonings if necessary (when it sits in the refrigerator for a long time the flavor of the vinegar may become muted), then spoon the lentils on top of greens. Sprinkle the feta over the lentils and serve the salad cold or at room temperature.

VEGETABLE PÂTÉ

Makes 2½ cups; about 6 servings

Pâté is traditionally made of mixed meats that are ground together and then baked into a loaf, something like a sophisticated meatloaf. We call this "pâté," but it's really more of a mock chicken liver. It's a dish I picked up from the kosher dairy restaurants that used to dot the area, and it's very easy to make, thanks to the food processor, and the fact that it doesn't need to be cooked, just chilled. Though we never served canned green beans as a side dish at Veselka, we do use them in our vegetable pâté, because you want very soft, almost overcooked green beans anyway. You can make your own from scratch, but be sure to boil them until they are almost meltingly soft with no snap left in them at all.

1 tablespoon olive oil

1 small onion, diced

1 garlic clove, diced

½ teaspoon salt

¼ teaspoon freshly ground black pepper

One 14 ½-ounce can cut green beans, drained and rinsed (about 2 cups)

4 hard-boiled eggs, peeled

1½ cups walnuts, toasted

1. In a medium sauté pan, heat the olive oil and sauté the onion and garlic until slightly golden in color and soft, about 10 minutes. Season with salt and pepper. Set aside until completely cool.

2. In a food processor fitted with a metal blade, combine the onion, garlic, green beans, eggs, and walnuts. Process until the mixture has formed a completely smooth paste and is thoroughly combined.

3. Transfer the mixture to a bowl, cover tightly with plastic wrap or a lid, and refrigerate for at least 2 hours to chill thoroughly. Taste the pâté before serving and add more salt and pepper, if necessary.

COLESLAW

Serves 6

At Veselka, we serve coleslaw with many of our sandwiches. We make a big batch of it every day, and we like it extra-tangy. Coleslaw will taste better if it sits in the refrigerator for a few hours.

½ head fresh white cabbage, finely shredded

1 small white onion

1 small carrot

¾ cup sour cream

¾ cup buttermilk

¾ cup mayonnaise

Salt

Freshly ground black pepper

1. Using a cleaver, shred the cabbage very fine. Slice the onion paper-thin. (A mandoline is very useful for this if you have one.) Shred the carrot on the largest holes of a box grater or in a food processor fitted with the grating blade.
2. In a medium bowl, combine the cabbage, onion, and carrot.
3. In a small bowl or measuring cup, whisk together the sour cream, buttermilk, and mayonnaise.
4. Pour the sour cream mixture over the vegetables and stir with a wooden spoon to combine thoroughly. Season to taste with salt and pepper. Serve cold.

SAUERKRAUT

Serves 4

Sauerkraut is something like sourdough—you keep it going in a long chain by adding more cabbage for fermentation. But you have to start somewhere, so we suggest you begin with 3 cups of store-bought sauerkraut, the more natural the better (see Resources on page 248). After that, you'll never have to buy sauerkraut again unless you want to. (Of course, sauerkraut must be refrigerated and it won't literally last indefinitely—if it looks or smells at all questionable, toss it and start over. If you're into canning foods, can sauerkraut for long-term storage.)

1 small onion, sliced

2 carrots, peeled and grated on the largest holes of a box grater

¼ head white or green cabbage, thinly shredded (1 to 2 cups)

3 cups sauerkraut

2 whole allspice berries

8 whole black peppercorns

Salt, if needed

1. Combine all the ingredients in a medium pot.
2. Add enough water to cover. Bring to a boil, then reduce the heat to low, and simmer gently until the vegetables have softened, 10 to 15 minutes.
3. Taste and add salt if desired. (The sauerkraut may be salty enough.)
4. Refrigerate at least 24 hours before serving.

CHICKEN SALAD

Serves 4

At Veselka, we poach boned chicken breasts to make our chicken salad, but if you have left-over roast chicken or boiled chicken left over after making Chicken Noodle Soup (page 18), feel free to use that.

2 small onions

3 celery stalks

4 boneless and skinless chicken breasts

1 carrot, chopped

1 parsnip, chopped

2 bay leaves

4 whole allspice berries

1 red bell pepper, seeded and diced

1½ cups mayonnaise

Salt

Freshly ground black pepper

1. Roughly chop 1 onion and 2 stalks of celery.
2. Place the chicken breasts, chopped onion, chopped celery, carrot, parsnip, bay leaves, and allspice berries in a medium pot and add enough cold water to cover. Bring to a boil, reduce the heat to low, and simmer until the chicken is cooked through, about 15 minutes.
3. Remove the chicken breasts from pot and set aside to cool. Discard the cooked vegetables. While the chicken is cooling, dice the remaining onion and the remaining celery stalk and set aside.
4. Once the chicken is cool enough to handle, shred it by hand into a large bowl.
5. To the bowl with the chicken, add the diced onion and celery, the bell pepper, and the mayonnaise. Stir with a large spoon to combine and season to taste with salt and pepper.
6. Chill thoroughly before serving.

TUNA SALAD

Serves 6

I think tuna salad is one of those foods like a hamburger—the way you ate it as a child always tastes best. I ate mine with a little Hellmann's mayonnaise and some crunchy bits of celery and onion, and that's how we make it at the restaurant.

3 cups chunk white tuna packed in water,
  well drained
1 small onion, minced
2 celery stalks, minced

½ cup mayonnaise
1 tablespoon coarsely ground black
  pepper

1. In a medium bowl, flake the tuna with a fork.
2. Add the onion, celery, and mayonnaise. Stir to combine, season with the black pepper, and stir again. Taste and adjust seasoning. (Most canned tuna is salty enough that you won't need additional salt.)
3. Chill completely before serving.

Variation: *For Turkey Salad, use 3 cups of roasted white meat turkey, shredded by hand, in place of the tuna.*

EGG SALAD

Serves 6

Our egg salad is the simplest there is—just eggs, mayonnaise, mustard, salt, and pepper. Yet, like our Oatmeal (page 225), it gets raves. To hard-boil eggs, place them in a pot and fill with cold water to cover. Bring to a boil, reduce the heat, and simmer for 15 minutes. After 15 minutes, dunk the cooked eggs in ice water to keep them from discoloring. That way your egg salad will look as good as it tastes.

12 large eggs, hard-boiled

½ cup mayonnaise

1 tablespoon Dijon mustard

Salt

Freshly ground black pepper

1. Chop the eggs, if possible with a wire egg slicer. Slice the egg once, then turn and slice in the other direction.

2. In a medium bowl, combine the chopped eggs, mayonnaise, and mustard. Fold gently with a fork or spatula to combine. Season to taste with salt and pepper.

3. Chill thoroughly before serving.

POTATO SALAD

Serves 8

The potato salad we serve at Veselka is 100 percent American. It's the kind you probably ate at picnics as a kid, and it still tastes pretty great on a hot summer day.

5 pounds Idaho potatoes, peeled and cut
    into 1-inch cubes
1 small carrot, cut into ½-inch dice
2 tender young leeks, white part only,
    minced (about ½ cup)
1 small onion, minced
1 celery stalk, minced

2 tablespoons chopped fresh dill
2 tablespoons chopped fresh flat-leaf
    parsley
1¾ cups mayonnaise
Salt
Freshly ground black pepper

1. Place the potatoes in a medium pot and add cold water to cover. Bring to a boil, reduce the heat to low, and simmer until the potatoes are tender, but not soft or dissolving, 15 to 20 minutes. (Test the potatoes with a knife, but don't do it too frequently, or they will get waterlogged.)

2. Meanwhile, place the diced carrot in a small pot and add cold water to cover. Bring to a boil and cook until the carrots have softened but still have some resistance, about 10 minutes. Immediately drain and rinse with cold water. Drain and set aside.

3. When the potatoes are cooked, drain them and spread them on a platter or jelly-roll pan to cool.

4. When the potatoes are completely cool, transfer them to a medium bowl. Add the blanched carrot, the leeks, onion, celery, dill, and parsley. Add the mayonnaise and stir gently with a spoon or spatula to combine.

5. Season to taste with salt and pepper and chill completely before serving. (You may want to taste and reseason the Potato Salad once it is chilled.)

MASHED POTATOES

Serves 6

Mashed potatoes are a great fit with any hearty entrée, especially a stew like Beef Stroganoff (page 61) or Ola's Famous Veal Goulash (page 60). The best way to make mashed potatoes is by hand, using either an old-fashioned potato masher or simply a fork. A food processor will actually purée the potatoes too *much and turn them gluey. At Veselka we use Idaho potatoes, but any variety will work.*

6 medium Idaho potatoes	6 tablespoons unsalted butter
½ cup heavy cream	Salt
½ cup whole milk	Freshly ground black pepper

1. Peel the potatoes and cut them in half. Place the potatoes in a large stockpot and add cold water to cover. Bring to a boil and cook until the potatoes are easily pierced with a fork or the tip of a paring knife but are not disintegrating, about 20 minutes. Meanwhile, in a separate small pot, heat the cream and milk gently, until small bubbles form at the edges and steam rises from the surface, but do not bring to a boil. Keep warm.

2. When the potatoes are cooked, drain them and then immediately return them to the same pot. (You want the pot to be warm.)

3. Cut the butter into a few pieces and add to the potatoes. Begin mashing the potatoes in the pot, off the heat, with a fork or potato masher, while gradually pouring in the cream and milk. Season to taste with generous amounts of salt and pepper and serve immediately. If the mashed potatoes cool too much as you are mashing them, return the pot to medium heat for a few minutes while whisking in additional milk or cream.

POTATO PANCAKES

Makes 10 large pancakes; 10 servings

These potato pancakes represent another ingenious Ukrainian use of some of the simplest ingredients. Peel and shred the potatoes on the largest holes of a box grater or in a food processor fitted with the shredding blade just before using them to prevent discoloring. The durum flour (sometimes sold as semolina flour) holds up better to frying than regular all-purpose flour would. These are great as a side dish, served with some sour cream, but cut into wedges and topped with dollops of sour cream (and maybe a little diced smoked salmon) they also make a good hors d'oeuvre.

1 small onion

1 garlic clove

3 pounds (about 4 medium) Idaho
   potatoes

2 large eggs, lightly beaten

2 teaspoons salt, plus more to taste

½ cup durum (semolina) flour

Vegetable oil, for frying

Freshly ground black pepper

Sour cream

1. Combine the onion and garlic in the bowl of a food processor fitted with the metal blade. Pulse a few times until very finely ground, almost puréed. Set aside.

2. Peel the potatoes, then grate them on the largest holes of a box grater or in a food processor fitted with the shredding blade. Do not place them in water.

3. In a large bowl, combine the onion and garlic, the potatoes, the eggs, and the 2 teaspoons salt. Mix with your hands. Add the flour in small amounts, about 1 tablespoon at a time, mixing to combine between additions. Depending on how wet the potatoes are, how large the eggs are, and even the weather, you may not need all the flour. The goal is a mixture that is moist but neither soupy nor overly dry. Stop when you have added enough flour.

4. Fill a large cast-iron skillet or large sauté pan with oil so that it comes about ½ inch up the sides of the skillet and heat the oil to 325°F. It should be very hot but not smoking. If you are not sure if the oil is hot enough, drop a small spoonful of the potato mixture into the skillet to test. It should start to sizzle immediately.

5. When the oil is hot, drop spoonfuls of the potato mixture (an average large skillet will hold 4 at a time) into the oil and cook until crispy on the bottom, about 3 minutes.

6. Flip the pancakes and cook until the other side is also golden brown and crispy.

7. Remove the cooked pancakes with a slotted spatula and drain on paper towels or brown paper bags. Add a little bit of oil to the skillet if you need to to bring it back to ½ inch up the side of the pan, reheat the oil, then repeat with the remaining potato batter.

8. Taste and season the potato pancakes with additional salt (if necessary—it may not be) and freshly ground pepper to taste. Serve hot with sour cream on the side.

HOME FRIED POTATOES

Serves 4 to 6

Home fried potatoes are a diner favorite, but they're relatively easy to make at home (hence the name, probably), and a great way to use up leftover boiled potatoes. These make a wonderful side dish for omelets and other egg dishes.

4 large Idaho potatoes, peeled

2 tablespoons vegetable oil or unsalted butter or a combination of the two

1 small onion, chopped

1 tablespoon paprika

Salt

Freshly ground black pepper

1. Place the peeled potatoes in a medium saucepan. Add cold water to cover. Bring to a boil and cook until the potatoes are cooked through but still very firm, 15 to 20 minutes.

2. Drain the potatoes and set aside to cool briefly. When they are cool enough to handle, slice the potatoes crosswise into rounds. If they are very large potatoes, cut the rounds into semicircles.

3. Heat a griddle or cast-iron skillet over medium heat.

4. Heat the oil and/or melt the butter on the surface of the griddle or skillet and add the potato slices and onion. Sprinkle with the paprika and season with salt and pepper.

5. Cook, turning and stirring occasionally with a spatula, until both the onions and the potatoes are browned, about 10 minutes. Taste and adjust seasoning and serve immediately.

KASHA

Serves 4

Kasha is a common side dish in Eastern Europe. It is made with buckwheat groats or kernels. At Veselka we use the Wolff's brand of kasha, which honestly is the only brand I've ever seen on grocery store shelves. It comes ground or in whole groats. We like the texture of the whole groats, but any of them will give you that nutty buckwheat flavor. Use kasha in place of rice—it's one of those rare foods that's both delicious and very good for you.

1 tablespoon unsalted butter

Salt

1 cup whole kasha

1 large egg, lightly beaten

Freshly ground black pepper

1. In a small pot, combine 2 cups water, the butter, and salt to taste. Bring to a boil.
2. When the water mixture is boiling, heat a medium sauté pan with a tight-fitting lid over medium heat.
3. In a small bowl, combine the kasha and egg. Add the kasha mixture to the dry pan and cook, stirring constantly, until the egg has dried and the kasha kernels are separate, about 3 minutes.
4. Carefully pour the boiling water into the pan, stir to combine, and cover. Simmer over low heat until all the liquid has been absorbed and the kasha is tender, about 10 minutes for whole kasha. Fluff with a fork, season to taste with pepper and additional salt if needed, and serve immediately.

MACARONI AND CHEESE

Serves 6 to 8

If you came of age in the pre-pasta era, you likely grew up eating, and loving, macaroni and cheese. If sales of macaroni and cheese at Veselka are any kind of indication, you probably still love it. We make our macaroni and cheese with little elbow macaroni and a crisp bread crumb topping. We use a light hand with the bread crumbs, but you can add more if you prefer. This can be prepared ahead of time and then baked just before serving.

3 cups elbow macaroni, about ¾ pound

4 cups whole milk

1 cup half-and-half

4 tablespoons unsalted butter

½ cup all-purpose flour

1½ teaspoons dried mustard

1 pound white Vermont cheddar, grated

1 teaspoon freshly ground black pepper

1 teaspoon salt

3 tablespoons panko (Japanese-style bread crumbs)

1. Preheat the oven to 350°F. Bring a large pot of lightly salted water to a boil and cook the macaroni, stirring occasionally, until tender, about 8 minutes. Drain and transfer to a 2-quart casserole dish.

2. In a small pot, combine the milk and half-and-half and heat until warm but not boiling. Meanwhile, in a large pot, melt the butter. Stir in the flour and dried mustard and cook, stirring constantly, until thickened but not browned, 2 to 3 minutes.

3. Pour the hot milk mixture into the flour and butter mixture, whisking constantly to avoid lumps. Bring to a boil over medium heat, whisking constantly so the bottom of the pot does not scorch. When the mixture has thickened and a few bubbles indicate that it is boiling, remove from the heat and stir in about three-quarters of the cheese a little at a time, stirring to combine between additions. Stir in the salt and pepper.

4. Pour the cheese sauce over the macaroni and stir to combine. Smooth the macaroni in the casserole so that it is of even thickness. Sprinkle the remaining grated cheese on top, then sprinkle on the panko. Bake in the preheated oven until the top is golden brown and bubbling, about 20 minutes.

5

DESSERTS

Black and White Cookies

Chocolate Chip Cookies

Peanut Butter Chocolate Chip
  Cookies

Oatmeal Raisin Cookies

M&M Cookies

Rice Krispie Treats

Raspberry-Apricot Bars

Brownies

Dream Bars

Rugelach

Biscotti

Rice Pudding

Baked Chocolate Custard

Vanilla Cupcakes

Banana Chocolate Chip Cupcakes

Chocolate Cupcakes

Buttercream Frosting

Mini Lemon Bundt Cakes

Ukrainian Poppy Seed Cake

Carrot Cake

Ukrainian Apple Crumb Cake

Sour Cream Cheesecake

Apple Pies

Cherry Crumb Pies

Blueberry Tarts

Banana Cream Pies

Peanut Butter Pies

Triple Chocolate Mousse Tart

Peanut Butter Doggie Biscuits

DESSERTS AT VESELKA fit into one of two categories: traditional Ukrainian or traditional American. All are extremely homey versions of comfort food. Ukrainians aren't big on serving dessert after a meal (with the exception of big holiday feasts), so many of the Ukrainian choices are not-too-sweet cakes and puddings that are perfect accompaniments to a cup of tea or coffee. They're intended to provide a sweet moment, usually shared with a friend, in the middle of the afternoon. Our American desserts include some showstoppers, but also include the sweet treats you probably loved as a kid, like cupcakes and chocolate chip cookies.

Many of the American desserts on our menu were brought to Veselka by our pastry chef, Lisa Straub, and Lisa learned many of them from her own mother, a meticulous home baker. You might be surprised to learn that Lisa is a highly trained chef with a degree from the Culinary Institute of America, this country's top cooking school. In fact, when I was looking for a new pastry chef eight or nine years ago and Lisa sent in her résumé, I moved it out of the pile of potential applicants, not because it didn't impress me, but because it intimidated me. She'd worked for more than a decade with high-end New York City restaurateur Larry Forgione and had been pastry chef at his elegant Beekman Tavern up in Rhinebeck, New York. But instinct told me that she might be a good fit, and I was right. Moving her résumé back into the pile of people to call was a smart move, and Lisa is a really important member of the Veselka team.

The "culture clash" does rear its head sometimes, however. In 2000 and 2001, Lisa competed in the U.S. Pastry Competition, which is a very big deal if you're

Our front glass counter display holds an array of desserts available at Veselka. *(Ben Fink)* Veselka pastry chef Lisa Straub holds a mouthwatering tray of her Boston Cream Pies. *(Ben Fink)*

a pastry chef. She worked in the Veselka kitchen to make cakes and sugar sculptures, which was not easy, given that the restaurant is open twenty-four hours a day and therefore the kitchen is busy twenty-four hours a day as well. Our bread baker is a big Polish guy named Zenic who's very sweet, but he didn't exactly appreciate the skill that goes into something like that, and he accidentally knocked down Lisa's work and didn't get why I was making such a big deal out of it. When the competition came around, though, at my suggestion he went to see what it was all about. He got dressed up in a suit and tie, and when he saw Lisa there doing her thing and understood the kind of work that goes into that type of project, he went up to her with tears in his eyes and apologized.

Lisa grew up on Long Island, baking with her mother, and she has a quality that the finest pastry chefs all seem to share: She's extremely well-organized. "If you stay organized, it's not stressful," Lisa says. She also says she loves working at Veselka because it's "a regular place to come and get really great food." It's a good thing she likes Veselka, because she spends a lot of time here—Lisa starts baking between 5:00 and 6:00 A.M. and leaves around 1:00 P.M.

Because the desserts and many of the baked goods for breakfasts, such as muffins, which are also Lisa's responsibility, are home-style, Lisa uses lots of her own mother's recipes, like the one for Sour Cream Cheesecake (page 143). At Veselka, however, Lisa makes many of the desserts in single servings. Not only does everyone love getting his or her own little pie or cake, but it cuts down on waste. Lisa loves getting to know customers and making special treats for them—once when a woman sitting at the counter commented that she liked our Cherry Crumb Pie (page 147), but her taste in fruit ran more to apples, Lisa asked her to wait twenty minutes and ran down to the kitchen to bake an apple version just for her. That's true customer service!

Little Ukraine

While the East Village neighborhood where Veselka stands is not the Ukrainian-American mecca it once was, it still has a number of Ukrainian institutions. Andy Lastowecky is a long-time Veselka customer and grew up in the area. Andy remembers that kids in the neighborhood went to public school during the week, but attended Ukrainian school on Saturdays, where they studied the language, as well as Ukrainian music and dancing. Everyone was a member of Plast, the Ukrainian scouting organization that still has headquarters upstairs. Andy has been involved with Plast since he was five years old.

"My wife and I both grew up in Plast," he says. "If you asked kids in the neighborhood what their number one activity was, it was always Plast. After school we would go up there and gather and play ping pong. After our activities upstairs, we'd come down to Veselka and buy candy or have an egg cream. Then Mr. Darmochwal opened up what we called 'the blue room,' which was for Ukrainians only. As I got

The Plast coat of arms intertwines the fleur-de-lis symbol of all scouting with the Ukrainian Trident. *(Plast Ukrainian Scouting Organization USA)*

Veselka founder Wolodymyr Darmochwal and his loyal German shepherd, Bura, who spent many days and evenings at the restaurant. *(Mykola Darmochwal)*

older, I became a Plast counselor and my wife—not yet my wife then—was in charge of the girls' program. He'd call upstairs and say, 'It's ten o'clock, come down and eat something.' Then he'd give us blintzes and varenyky. He knew we didn't have the big bucks. He was a person who worked very hard. He was here all the time with his dog, a German shepherd named Bura. Sometimes he would fall asleep in the middle of a conversation. All of a sudden you'd be answering him and you'd realize he was snoring."

Andy moved out of the neighborhood a few years ago, but it had changed long before that, he says. The wave of Ukrainian immigrants that arrived in the East Village after the Second World War has dispersed, replaced with a more recent, post-liberation wave of Ukrainian immigrants here for economic rather than political reasons. "Back in the 1970s, if you came here on a Friday night, there would be easily one hundred kids out on the street, hanging out in front of Plast and Veselka," says Andy. "These days, the crowd is standing in front of our credit union at 108 Second Avenue. The new immigrants are very different."

It's true that many of the Ukrainian institutions in the neighborhood have closed. There used to be three or four Ukrainian butchers in the area, but now Julian Baczynsky's East Village Meat Market (page 67) is the only one left. Orchidia, an Italian-Ukrainian place that served pizza with kielbasa and another pizza called the Garbage Pie, was across the street at Second Avenue and 9th Street until it closed in 1984. The Ukrainian bookstore Arka on 7th Street has moved to 89 East 2nd Street, but it doesn't have much space for books and magazines in its new location and stocks mostly embroidered blouses. The headquarters of the Ukrainian Communist Party in New York used to be on East 4th Street, but they've been shut down, and in their place there is the ironically named KGB Bar.

But there are several Ukrainian institutions still going strong in the neighborhood, all in close proximity to each other. Consider the following brief Ukrainian historical walking tour, ending with a plate of pierogi at Veselka.

WALKING TOUR

Start at the **Ukrainian Museum** on East 6th Street between Second and Third avenues. This small museum stages art and cultural exhibitions relating to Ukrainian heritage, covering everything from folkloric clothing to maps to traditional portraits of historic figures. The permanent collection includes Easter eggs and ceramics, as well as large amounts of work by artists like Nikifor and Vasyl Krychevsky. A small gift shop sells cards, books, jewelry, and more.

Walk one block north to **St. George Ukrainian Catholic Church** on the corner of 7th Street and Taras Shevchenko Place, named for the renowned Ukrainian writer. The church celebrated its first mass in 1905 (at a different location), and it remains a gathering spot for the Ukrainian community. Many parishioners travel in from the suburbs every Sunday for both mass and socializing. The current building was built in 1978 in classic Byzantine style. A cupola rests on top, and mosaics on the facade depict both Jesus and Ukrainians in native costume. On Fridays, the church sells borscht and pierogi in the basement to raise funds.

From there, cross the street to **Surma** at 11 East 7th Street. Surma sells traditional Ukrainian crafts such as hand-woven carpets, hand-painted icons, and wooden eggs (as well as real chicken eggs), and ceramics. It also stocks CDs and videos of traditional Ukrainian music and dancing, books and magazines, and honey and other food products. Beautiful flowing hand-embroidered blouses can be ordered either at the store or on its Web site, as can hand-tooled leather *opanky* moccasins.

In the market for some kielbasa or incredible housemade deli meats? Stop at Julian Baczynsky's **East Village Meat Market**, 139 Second Avenue, between St. Mark's Place and 9th Street. (See page 67 for more on East Village Meat Market.)

Walk up the half-block to 9th Street, cross Second Avenue, and you're right outside the door to **Veselka.** Refuel with pierogi. Смачного!

1. The Ukrainian Museum

    222 East 6th Street

    Tel 212-228-0110

    www.ukrainianmuseum.org

2. St. George Ukrainian Catholic Church

    30 East 7th Street

    Tel 212-674-1615

    www.brama.com/stgeorge

3. Surma

    11 East 7th Street

    Tel 212-477-0729

    www.surmastore.com

4. East Village Meat Market

    139 Second Avenue

    Tel 212-228-5590

5. Veselka

    144 Second Avenue

    Tel 212-228-9682

    www.veselka.com

East Village Ukrainian Historical Walking Tour

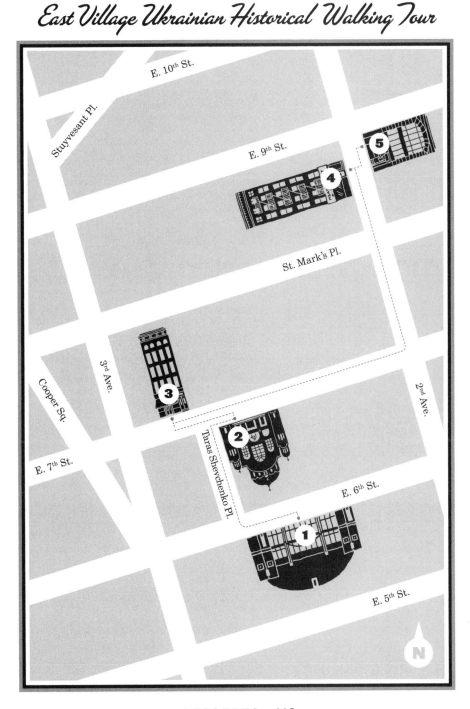

BLACK AND WHITE COOKIES

Makes 18 large cookies

These cakelike yin-and-yang treats are a New York City classic. Be sure to use cake flour and not regular all-purpose flour or the cookies will be unbearably dense. The dough is too wet to be rolled and cut. Instead it is piped through a pastry tube (if you don't have a pastry bag, substitute a large ziplock plastic bag with one corner cut off). For the icing, a good quality chocolate is everything. At the restaurant, we use Callebaut.

DOUGH

1¾ cups sugar

16 tablespoons (8 ounces) vegetable shortening

6 large eggs

1 tablespoon vanilla extract

6 cups cake flour

1 tablespoon plus 1½ teaspoons baking powder

1½ teaspoons salt

1 cup milk

ICING

1 pound fondant

10 ounces semisweet chocolate

1. Preheat the oven to 375°F. Line three cookie sheets with parchment paper and set aside.

2. In the large bowl of a stand mixer (or in a large bowl using a handheld mixer), cream together the sugar and shortening until light and fluffy, about 3 minutes. Beat in the eggs and vanilla.

3. In a medium bowl, whisk together the flour, baking powder, and salt.

4. Add about one-third of the flour mixture to the shortening mixture and beat to combine, then about one-third of the milk and beat to combine. Continue to alternate with two more additions, beating smooth between additions, until the flour mixture and milk have been incorporated.

5. Using a pastry tube fitted with a round piping tip or a large ziplock plastic bag with one corner cut off, pipe out cookies about 2 inches in diameter onto the prepared cookie sheets.

6. Place the cookie sheets in the oven and reduce the oven temperature to 350°F. Bake the cookies for 5 minutes at 350°F, then reduce the oven temperature to 325°F. Bake until the bottoms of the cookies are golden and the tops are firm, 10 to 12 minutes.

7. Slide the parchment paper with the cookies to racks and allow the cookies to cool completely.

8. To decorate the cookies, divide the fondant in half. Place half of the fondant and the chocolate in a microwave-safe bowl and the other half of the fondant in a separate microwave-safe bowl. Microwave on low power until melted and smooth, about 30 seconds to 1 minute. (You may need to stop and stir them a few times, then return them to the microwave. Time will vary depending on your microwave.) Stir the chocolate and fondant to combine thoroughly.

9. If necessary, add a little water to either or both batches of fondant to achieve a spreadable but still thick consistency. Using a small metal offset spatula, spread one half of each cookie with the white fondant. (It may be helpful to use a butter knife to mark a very shallow line down the center of each cookie before you start.) With a clean spatula, spread the other half of each cookie with the chocolate fondant. Set aside and allow the fondant to cool and set.

CHOCOLATE CHIP COOKIES

Makes 16 large cookies

Is there a better cookie in the world than a chocolate chip cookie? I don't think so, and though there are dozens of recipes for chocolate chip cookies out there, I think these are the best I've ever had—neither too crispy nor too soft, with just the right amount of chocolate chips and the crunch of walnuts.

24 tablespoons (3 sticks) unsalted butter, softened

¾ cup plus 2 tablespoons brown sugar, firmly packed

1 cup granulated sugar

3 large eggs

2 teaspoons vanilla extract

2¾ cups all-purpose flour

1¼ teaspoons baking soda

1½ teaspoons salt

¾ teaspoon ground cinnamon

14 ounces (about 2⅓ cups) chocolate chips

12 ounces (about 2¼ cups) chopped walnuts, toasted

1. Preheat the oven to 350°F. Line three large cookie sheets with parchment paper. Set aside.
2. In the large bowl of a stand mixer (or in a large bowl using a handheld mixer), cream together the butter and sugars until light and fluffy, about 3 minutes.
3. Add the eggs to the mixture one at a time, blending until combined, scraping down the sides of the bowl with a spatula between additions. Mix in the vanilla.
4. In a medium bowl, whisk together the flour, baking soda, salt, and cinnamon.
5. Add the flour mixture and beat just until fully incorporated. With a spatula, fold in the chocolate chips and walnuts.
6. To form each cookie, use a 4-ounce ice cream scoop to drop dough onto the prepared cookie sheets, leaving about 3 inches between cookies on all sides.
7. Bake until the cookies are lightly browned, about 12 minutes. (Depending on the size of your oven, you may have to do this in batches.)
8. Slide the parchment paper with the cookies onto racks to cool.

PEANUT BUTTER CHOCOLATE CHIP COOKIES

Makes 14 large cookies

I think the chocolate chips take these cookies from merely excellent to sublime, but if you don't like chocolate with your peanut butter (hard to imagine), you can simply leave them out.

16 tablespoons (2 sticks) unsalted butter,
  softened
1 cup plus 1 tablespoon granulated sugar
1 cup brown sugar, firmly packed
1 cup crunchy peanut butter

4 large eggs
2½ cups all-purpose flour
½ teaspoon baking soda
½ teaspoon salt
1 cup semisweet chocolate chips

1. In the large bowl of a stand mixer (or in a large bowl using a handheld mixer), cream together the butter, 1 cup granulated sugar, and brown sugar until light and fluffy, about 3 minutes. Beat in the peanut butter.
2. Add 2 of the eggs to the mixture and blend until combined. Stop and scrape down the sides of the bowl with a spatula. Add the remaining 2 eggs and blend until combined. Stop and scrape down the sides of the bowl with a spatula.
3. In a medium bowl, whisk together the flour, baking soda, and salt.
4. Add the flour mixture to the peanut butter mixture and beat until the flour mixture has all been incorporated. With a spatula, fold in the chocolate chips. Chill the dough for at least 1 hour, or as long as overnight.
5. When you're ready to bake the cookies, preheat the oven to 350°F. Line three large cookie sheets with parchment paper.
6. To form each cookie, use a 4-ounce ice cream scoop to drop dough onto the prepared cookie sheets, leaving about 3 inches between cookies on all sides.
7. Press the top of each cookie with a fork to flatten and imprint the top with lines. Sprinkle the remaining 1 tablespoon of sugar over the cookies. Bake until the cookies are firm, about 12 minutes. (Depending on the size of your oven, you may have to do this in batches. If so, return remaining dough to the refrigerator for the interim.)
8. Slide the parchment paper with the cookies onto racks to cool.

OATMEAL RAISIN COOKIES

Makes 10 large cookies

Typical oatmeal cookies with raisins and walnuts have a tendency to be a little dense and heavy. At Veselka, we use coconut rather than nuts and we use low-protein cake flour in the cookies, which gives them a lighter texture.

16 tablespoons (2 sticks) unsalted butter,
  softened

1 teaspoon vanilla extract

¾ cup brown sugar, firmly packed

¼ cup plus 3 tablespoons granulated sugar

2 large eggs

2 cups cake flour

1 cup rolled oats

1 cup shredded sweetened coconut

1 teaspoon baking powder

1 teaspoon baking soda

¼ teaspoon salt

½ teaspoon ground cinnamon

1 cup raisins

1. Preheat the oven to 350°F. Line two large cookie sheets with parchment paper. Set aside.

2. In the large bowl of a stand mixer (or in a large bowl using a handheld mixer), cream together the butter, vanilla, and sugars until light and fluffy, about 3 minutes.

3. Add the eggs to the mixture one at a time, blending until combined, then scraping down the sides of the bowl with a spatula between additions.

4. In a medium bowl, whisk together the flour, oats, coconut, baking powder, baking soda, salt, and cinnamon.

5. Add the flour mixture to the butter mixture and beat until the flour mixture has all been incorporated. With a spatula, fold in the raisins.

6. To form each cookie, use a 4-ounce ice cream scoop to drop dough onto the prepared cookie sheets, leaving about 3 inches between cookies on all sides.

7. Bake until the cookies are lightly browned, about 12 minutes.

8. Slide the parchment paper with the cookies onto racks to cool.

M&M COOKIES

Makes 14 large cookies

I've seen more than one white-haired customer turn virtually childlike when handed a cookie packed with M&Ms.

16 tablespoons (2 sticks) unsalted butter, softened

¾ cup granulated sugar

¾ cup brown sugar, firmly packed

1 teaspoon vanilla extract

2 large eggs

2¼ cups all-purpose flour

1 teaspoon baking soda

½ teaspoon salt

2 cups chocolate chips

1½ cups plain M&M candies

1. Preheat the oven to 350°F. Line three large cookie sheets with parchment paper. Set aside.

2. In the large bowl of a stand mixer (or in a large bowl using a handheld mixer), cream together the butter, sugars, and vanilla until light and fluffy, about 3 minutes.

3. Add the eggs to the mixture one at a time, blending until combined, then scraping down the sides of the bowl with a spatula between additions.

4. In a medium bowl, whisk together the flour, baking soda, and salt.

5. Add the flour mixture to the butter mixture and beat until incorporated. With a spatula, fold in the chocolate chips and about 1¼ cups of the M&M candies.

6. To form each cookie, use a 4-ounce ice cream scoop to drop dough onto the prepared cookie sheets, leaving about 4 inches between cookies on all sides. Place the remaining ¼ cup of M&M candies on top of the cookies (about 3 per cookie) and press them gently into the dough. (This makes the cookies prettier, but if you prefer, you can simply fold in all the M&M candies in step 5.)

7. Bake until cookies are lightly browned, about 12 minutes. (Depending on the size of your oven, you may have to do this in batches.)

8. Slide the parchment paper with the cookies onto racks to cool.

RICE KRISPIE TREATS

Makes 12 large squares

If you grew up in the United States, chances are these sweet, crunchy, sticky bars were one of the first things you ever made in the kitchen. They're still delicious, and probably even easier than they seemed back then. For added color, we mix in a handful of colored sprinkles.

Vegetable oil cooking spray, for pan and bowl

1 pound mini marshmallows

3 tablespoons unsalted butter

10 cups Rice Krispies cereal

1. Spray a 13×9-inch baking pan with vegetable oil cooking spray and set aside. Spray a large mixing bowl with vegetable oil cooking spray and set aside.

2. Reserve 1 cup of marshmallows. Place the remaining marshmallows and the butter in a microwave-safe bowl. Microwave 20 seconds at a time until soft and melted (about 2 minutes total).

3. Place the cereal and the remaining 1 cup of marshmallows in the mixing bowl sprayed with vegetable oil. Spray a rubber spatula with vegetable oil and use to mix in the melted marshmallows and butter until thoroughly combined.

4. Transfer the mixture to the sprayed pan. Allow to cool and set completely, then cut into 12 squares.

RASPBERRY-APRICOT BARS

Makes 12 large bars

With their alternating stripes of raspberry and apricot jam, these bars always remind me of stained glass. And they taste just as good as they look. You may end up with extra frangipane (the almond-paste mixture), depending on how large the lines you pipe are. It will keep in the refrigerator for a week or two.

CRUST

16 tablespoons (2 sticks) unsalted butter, softened

1 cup sugar

1 teaspoon vanilla extract

1 large egg

2⅔ cup all-purpose flour

FILLING

7 ounces almond paste

8 tablespoons (1 stick) butter

¼ teaspoon salt

⅔ cup plus 1 teaspoon sugar

3 large eggs

½ cup all-purpose flour

1 cup raspberry jam

1¼ cups apricot jam

1. To make the crust, in the large bowl of a stand mixer (or in a large bowl using a handheld mixer), cream together the butter, sugar, and vanilla until light and fluffy, about 3 minutes.

2. Add the egg and blend until combined, then scrape down the sides of the bowl with a spatula. Add the flour and mix until combined.

3. Wrap the dough in plastic wrap and refrigerate for at least 30 minutes.

4. Prepare a piece of parchment paper that is about 10 inches × 14 inches (it will need to line the bottom and sides of a 13×9-inch baking pan). Arrange the parchment on your work surface and place the dough on top of the parchment. Roll out the dough until it covers the surface of the parchment paper.

5. Transfer the parchment paper and dough to a 13×9-inch baking pan. Press the edges of the dough into an even rim that goes up the sides of the pan. Crimp the edges to create a decorative border. Refrigerate for at least 2 hours and as long as overnight.

6. When you are ready to bake the crust, preheat the oven to 350°F. Score the dough with a fork and bake until the surface is dry and light golden brown, about 20 minutes. Set the crust aside to cool in the pan. Leave the oven on, set to 350°F.

7. While the crust is cooling, prepare the frangipane: In the large bowl of a stand mixer (or in a large bowl using a handheld mixer), cream together the almond paste, butter, salt, and ⅔ cup sugar until light and fluffy.

8. Add the eggs one at a time, beating smooth between additions, and then stopping and scraping down the sides of the bowl. When all the eggs have been incorporated, beat in the flour. If the frangipane seems very soft, refrigerate it for 30 minutes or so until it is firm enough to be piped. (On a cool day this may not be necessary.)

9. Using a pastry bag fitted with a round tip or a ziplock plastic bag with one corner cut off, pipe diagonal lines of frangipane on the crust. Leave empty space between the lines of frangipane that is of a width about equal to the lines themselves.

10. Pipe raspberry jam and 1 cup apricot jam into the empty spaces, alternating the jams so that they form multicolored stripes. Return to the oven and bake until the jam and frangipane are set, 20 to 30 minutes. (This can vary widely depending on the jam you are using.) Remove the bars from oven and cool completely.

11. To glaze the bars, place the remaining ¼ cup apricot jam and remaining 1 teaspoon sugar in a small saucepan with 2 tablespoons water. Stir to combine, then bring the mixture to a boil (alternatively, microwave for approximately 1 minute). While it is still warm, pass it through a sieve and brush the resulting glaze onto the cooled bars. Allow the glaze to set, then cut into 12 bars.

BROWNIES

Makes 20 large brownies

The world seems to fall into two camps: Those who like nuts in their brownies, and those who do not. We are definitely on the nutty side at Veselka.

1 pound semisweet chocolate

24 tablespoons (3 sticks) unsalted butter

3 cups sugar

1 tablespoon vanilla extract

8 large eggs

1 teaspoon salt

2 cups all-purpose flour

2 cups chopped walnuts, toasted

1. Preheat the oven to 350°F. Line a 18×13×1½-inch jelly-roll pan with parchment paper, then spray with vegetable oil spray and set aside.

2. In a double boiler or a large, heat-proof bowl set over a pan of simmering water, melt the chocolate and butter until smooth. Set aside to cool for 5 minutes, then stir in the sugar and vanilla. Add the eggs 2 at a time, stirring smooth between additions. Stir in the salt and flour.

3. Pour the batter into the prepared pan. Sprinkle the walnuts on top.

4. Bake for 15 minutes, then reduce the oven temperature to 325°F and bake until the brownies are firm, about 20 additional minutes.

5. Cool the brownies in the pan. When the brownies are cool, cut them into 3-inch squares.

DREAM BARS

Makes 12 large bar cookies

I'm not sure where these bar cookies, which have a little bit of everything in them, originated—though I know they're not Ukrainian. These are very rich because of the condensed milk.

Vegetable oil cooking spray, for the pan

1½ cups graham cracker crumbs

10 tablespoons unsalted butter, melted

½ cup chocolate chips

½ cup shredded sweetened coconut

½ cup chopped walnuts

½ cup rolled oats

One 14-ounce can sweetened condensed milk

1. Preheat the oven to 350°F.
2. Spray a 7×7-inch square baking pan with vegetable oil cooking spray. In a small bowl, combine the graham cracker crumbs and the melted butter. Spread and press the mixture evenly into the bottom of the prepared pan to form a crust.
3. Sprinkle the chocolate chips, coconut, walnuts, and rolled oats over the crust. Pour the sweetened condensed milk over the top and bake in the preheated oven until light golden brown, 25 to 30 minutes.
4. Allow the bars to cool to room temperature in the pan, then chill in the refrigerator until very cold. Cut into 12 bars.

RUGELACH

Makes 16 rugelach

Rugelach are pastries made with cream cheese dough. They originated in Eastern Europe and may be filled with nuts, poppy seeds, chocolate, or jam, as they are here. I think either apricot or raspberry jam tastes best, but really you could use any flavor you like. A couple rolled-up rugelach are the perfect "something sweet" to serve with a cup of tea or coffee. By piping the jam down the center of the dough, you keep it from leaking out the sides, and that way you don't get burnt bits on the bottom of your rugelach.

16 tablespoons (2 sticks) unsalted butter, chilled

One 8-ounce package cream cheese, chilled

2 cups plus 2 tablespoons all-purpose flour

Vegetable oil cooking spray, for the pans

½ cup sour cream

½ cup apricot or raspberry jam

1 teaspoon ground cinnamon

2½ teaspoons sugar

½ cup graham cracker crumbs

¼ cup plus 1 tablespoon chopped walnuts (if using apricot jam), or ½ cup chocolate chips (if using raspberry jam)

Confectioners' sugar, for finishing (if using apricot jam) or melted chocolate, for finishing (if using raspberry jam)

1. Mix the butter, cream cheese, and flour by hand in a bowl or in a food processor fitted with the stainless steel blade until the dough forms a ball. Press the dough into a flat disk, wrap in plastic wrap, and refrigerate for at least 1 hour.

2. Preheat the oven to 350°F. Spray two 18×13×1½-inch jelly-roll pans with cooking spray, line with parchment paper, and set aside.

3. On a lightly floured surface, with a well-floured rolling pin, roll out the refrigerated dough into a strip about 4 inches wide, 34 inches long, and ¼ inch thick. Fold the dough in thirds from top to bottom, like a business letter. Lightly flour the surface, turn the dough 45 degrees, and again roll the dough into a strip 4 inches wide, 34 inches long, and ¼ inch thick.

4. Spread the sour cream in a thin layer over the dough, leaving ¼-inch border free of sour cream.

5. Using a metal offset spatula, spread the jam over the sour cream, still leaving a ¼-inch border clear. Sprinkle the sour cream with the cinnamon, sugar, and graham cracker crumbs. Sprinkle on the walnuts (if using apricot jam) or chocolate chips (if using raspberry jam) over the jam, concentrating most of them in the center, but covering the other areas lightly.

6. Fold the dough in thirds (like a business letter) over the strip of jam. You should now have a log of dough 34 inches long with the fillings inside. Using a hot, dry knife, cut the folded dough into 2½-inch-long rectangles. Wipe off the knife between cuts.

7. Transfer the rugelach to the prepared jelly-roll pans, leaving about 2 inches between them on all sides.

8. Bake the cookies at 350°F for 15 minutes. Reduce the oven temperature to 325°F and bake until golden brown, about 15 additional minutes.

9. Transfer parchment paper with the rugelach to racks to cool.

10. When the rugelach are cool, sprinkle apricot rugelach with confectioners' sugar or drizzle melted chocolate onto raspberry rugelach.

BISCOTTI

Makes 32 biscotti

The word "biscotti" means twice-cooked, which is what accounts for the satisfying crunch of these almond cookies. The first time you bake the dough in a log, and then you slice them and bake them again to dry the surface. They're perfect for dunking in a cup of coffee. These need a nice long session in the refrigerator before they're baked in order to have the right consistency, so be sure to start them the day before you want to serve them.

12 tablespoons (1½ sticks) unsalted butter, softened

1½ cups sugar

3 large eggs

3½ cups all-purpose flour

¾ teaspoon baking powder

¾ teaspoon baking soda

1¼ cups semi sweet chocolate chips

1¼ cups sliced almonds

1. Line two cookie sheets with parchment paper and set aside.

2. In the large bowl of a stand mixer (or in a large bowl using a handheld mixer), cream together the butter and sugar until light and fluffy, about 3 minutes.

3. Add the eggs to the mixture, blending until combined, then scrape down the sides of the bowl with a spatula

4. In a medium bowl, whisk together the flour, baking powder, and baking soda.

5. Add about one-third of the flour mixture to the butter mixture and mix until combined. Stop and scrape down the sides of the bowl with a spatula. Repeat with about half of the remaining flour mixture, and then the balance. Add the chocolate chips and almonds and mix just until they are evenly distributed.

6. Working on a lightly floured surface, use your hands to shape the dough into 2 logs, about 2 inches by 14 inches each. Place the dough on the prepared pans and refrigerate overnight.

7. The next day, preheat the oven to 350°F. Bake the logs until they are firm and golden brown, about 30 minutes.

8. Set the logs aside to cool and lower the oven temperature to 300°F. When the logs are just barely warm, use a serrated knife to slice them into ½-inch-wide biscotti.

9. Return the biscotti to the cookie sheets and return to the oven. Bake until the biscotti are golden brown and very crisp, about 10 minutes.

RICE PUDDING

Serves 8

As with all great comfort foods, I think everybody prefers the rice pudding he or she ate as a kid. At Veselka, we try to accommodate that by making a home-style rice pudding that's soft and sweet and flavored with cinnamon and vanilla. We make it with Italian Arborio rice, though, as it has more starch than most other types.

8 ounces (about 1 heaping cup) Arborio rice

2 cups whole milk

4 tablespoons (½ stick) unsalted butter

1 vanilla bean, split and seeds scraped

¼ cup plus 1 tablespoon sugar

1 cinnamon stick

1½ cups heavy cream

Ground cinnamon and sugar, for finishing

1. Place the rice in a medium saucepan and add 2 cups cold water. Bring to a boil, then reduce the heat and simmer gently until almost all of the water has been absorbed, about 15 minutes.

2. Add the milk, butter, vanilla bean and seeds, sugar, and cinnamon stick to the rice. Stir to combine and simmer until the rice is tender and about one-third of the liquid has evaporated, about 10 minutes.

3. Transfer the rice to a large serving bowl and add ½ cup of the heavy cream. Chill, stirring every 15 minutes, until the rice is completely cold and the liquid has thickened.

4. Remove and discard the cinnamon stick and vanilla bean. Whip the remaining 1 cup of heavy cream to soft peaks and gently fold the whipped cream into the rice. Return to refrigerator and chill until completely cold. Sprinkle with cinnamon and sugar just before serving.

BAKED CHOCOLATE CUSTARD

Makes six 8-ounce individual custards

As with almost any chocolate dessert, the tastiness of this baked custard will depend on the quality of the chocolate you use, so be sure to select a high-quality brand.

9 egg yolks

2 tablespoons coffee extract

1 quart heavy cream

¾ cup plus 2 tablespoons sugar

8 ounces semisweet chocolate, chopped

Whipped cream and chocolate shavings, for finishing

1. Preheat the oven to 325°F. Place the egg yolks in a heat-proof bowl and whisk in the coffee extract.
2. Combine the cream and sugar in a heavy-bottomed saucepan and bring to a boil. Add the chopped chocolate, whisk to dissolve, then remove the pan from the heat.
3. Add about 2 cups of the hot cream mixture to the egg yolk mixture and, working quickly, whisk vigorously. (If you don't act quickly, the egg will cook and curdle.)
4. Pour the tempered yolk mixture back into the saucepan and whisk again to combine.
5. When the ingredients are well incorporated, strain the mixture through a fine-mesh sieve, then pour the strained mixture into six 8-ounce ramekins (or oven-proof coffee mugs).
6. Arrange the custards in a water bath and bake in the preheated oven until set, 25 to 30 minutes. Remove the ramekins from the water bath and chill overnight before serving. Just before serving, top the custards with whipped cream and chocolate shavings.

VANILLA CUPCAKES

Makes 18 large cupcakes

Is there anything more satisfying than a moist vanilla cupcake? Without chocolate or banana or any fancy flavorings, I think vanilla cupcakes need to be supermoist, with a perfectly tender crumb.

18 tablespoons (2 sticks plus 2 tablespoons) unsalted butter, room temperature

1⅓ cups sugar

2 teaspoons vanilla extract

4 egg yolks

1 large egg

2 cups plus 2 tablespoons cake flour

¾ teaspoon baking powder

¾ teaspoon baking soda

½ teaspoon salt

¾ cup sour cream

1. Preheat the oven to 350°F. Place paper cupcake liners in 18 indentations in one or two nonstick muffin tins. Set aside.

2. In the large bowl of a stand mixer (or in a large bowl using a handheld mixer), cream together the butter, sugar, and vanilla until light and fluffy, about 3 minutes. Beat in the egg yolks two at a time, beating until combined between additions. Beat in the whole egg.

3. In a medium bowl, whisk together the flour, baking powder, baking soda, and salt.

4. Add about one-third of the flour mixture to the butter mixture and beat until smooth, then add about one-third of the sour cream and beat until smooth. Continue to alternate with two more additions of each, beating smooth between additions, until the flour mixture and sour cream have been incorporated.

5. Distribute the batter evenly among the liners in the prepared pans. Bake in the preheated oven until the cupcakes are lightly browned and a toothpick inserted in the center of one comes out dry, 15 to 20 minutes.

7. Cool the cupcakes in the pans on a rack for 5 minutes, then remove the cupcakes from the pan and transfer to rack to cool completely. Frost with Buttercream Frosting (page 135) if desired.

BANANA CHOCOLATE CHIP CUPCAKES

Makes 18 large cupcakes

One of the frustrating things about a restaurant like Veselka, where the customers feel so personally invested in the food and consider the restaurant "theirs," is that when you try to make even a tiny change, there may be an uprising. We once took these cupcakes off the menu in order to try out some new desserts. A week later, a letter arrived in the mail from a customer, pleading with us to put the cupcakes back on the menu and explaining that eating a banana chocolate chip cupcake from Veselka was a part of his daily routine and he was terribly upset by its absence! We put the cupcakes back on the menu. Make sure your bananas are very soft with lots of brown spots before you attempt this recipe. These are delicious either bare or with Buttercream Frosting (page 135).

16 tablespoons (2 sticks) unsalted butter, softened	4 large eggs
1½ cups brown sugar, firmly packed	4 cups all-purpose flour
1½ cups granulated sugar	1 teaspoon baking soda
2 tablespoons vanilla extract	½ teaspoon salt
6 overripe bananas, mashed with a fork	1 cup buttermilk
	1 cup semisweet chocolate chips

1. Preheat oven to 350°F. Place paper cupcake liners in 18 indentations in one or two nonstick muffin tins. Set aside.

2. In the large bowl of a stand mixer (or in a large bowl using a handheld mixer), cream together the butter, sugars, and vanilla until light and fluffy, about 3 minutes. Beat in the mashed bananas.

3. Add 2 of the eggs to the mixture and blend until combined. Stop the mixer and scrape down the sides of the bowl with a spatula. Add the remaining two eggs and blend until combined. Stop and scrape down the sides of the bowl again with a spatula.

4. In a medium bowl, whisk together the flour, baking soda, and salt.

5. Add about one-third of the flour mixture to the butter mixture and beat smooth, then add about one-third of the buttermilk and beat smooth. Continue to alternate with two more additions, beating smooth between additions, until the flour mixture and buttermilk have been incorporated. With a spatula, fold in the chocolate chips.

6. Distribute the batter evenly among the liners in the prepared pans. Bake in the preheated oven until the cupcakes are lightly browned and a toothpick inserted in the center comes out dry, 15 to 20 minutes.

7. Cool the cupcakes in the pans on a rack for 5 minutes, then remove the cupcakes from the pan and transfer to rack to cool completely. Frost with Buttercream Frosting if desired.

CHOCOLATE CUPCAKES

Makes 24 cupcakes

Like the Banana Chocolate Chip Cupcakes, these have their dedicated fans. We once ran out of the Valrhona cocoa powder that we normally use, and one customer noticed immediately and asked why his cupcake was "less chocolate-y than usual"! This recipe makes 24 cupcakes, and the cupcakes are large, but any extras freeze well—just be sure to wrap them tightly.

2¼ cups whole milk

1½ cups unsweetened cocoa powder,
   preferably Valrhona

3½ cups all-purpose flour

3¼ cups sugar

1 teaspoon baking soda

½ teaspoon salt

3 large eggs, lightly beaten

3 tablespoons vanilla extract

24 tablespoons (3 sticks) unsalted butter,
   melted and cooled

1. Preheat the oven to 350°F. Place paper cupcake liners in 24 indentations in two nonstick muffin tins. Set aside.

2. In a small saucepan over medium heat, warm the milk until it just comes to a boil. As soon as the first bubble appears on the surface, remove the milk from the heat and pour it into a large mixing bowl. (Alternatively, heat it in the microwave until hot but not boiling.) Immediately whisk in the cocoa powder until dissolved. Set aside to cool.

3. Meanwhile, in a medium bowl combine the flour, sugar, baking soda, and salt.

4. Once the milk mixture has cooled, whisk in the eggs and vanilla. Add the flour mixture to the milk mixture and stir until combined. Add the butter and stir until combined.

5. Distribute the batter evenly among the liners in the prepared pans. Bake the cupcakes in the preheated oven until a toothpick inserted in the center of one comes out dry, 15 to 20 minutes.

6. Cool the cupcakes in the pans on a rack for 5 minutes, then remove the cupcakes from the pan and transfer to rack to cool completely. Frost with Buttercream Frosting (page 135) if desired.

BUTTERCREAM FROSTING

Makes about 3 cups buttercream, enough for 24 cupcakes

This is the basic vanilla icing that we use on all of our cupcakes at Veselka.

6 egg whites (about ¾ cup)

1¾ cups sugar

1 pound (4 sticks) unsalted butter, room
temperature, cut into small pieces

1 tablespoon vanilla extract

1. Combine the egg whites and sugar in the large bowl of a stand mixer. (Though the egg whites won't come close to filling the bowl, they expand considerably as you make the buttercream, so be sure to start with a large bowl.) Set the bowl over a warm water bath and whisk by hand until all the sugar has dissolved. The mixture will warm somewhat, but do not let it get overly hot.

2. Place the bowl on the mixer fitted with the beaters and mix on high speed until cool, about 10 minutes. With the mixer still running, add a few pieces of butter at a time. Beat until thick, smooth, and shiny, 5 to 10 minutes, depending on the temperature of the room.

3. With the mixer still running, add the vanilla and mix until incorporated, about 1 minute.

4. Do not refrigerate buttercream. (If buttercream separates, it is too cold. Warm it gently over a water bath once again and beat on the mixer until it is again emulsified.)

MINI LEMON BUNDT CAKES

Makes 12 mini Bundt cakes

This is one of those Veselka recipes that seems deceptively simple, maybe even obvious. Chances are you've got a zillion recipes for a lemon Bundt cake. But this one is extra lemony because of the combination of juice and zest, and baking the cakes in mini Bundt pans means they're easy to freeze. That's what we look for in a dessert—a classic raised to a higher level. If you don't have a mini Bundt pan, use a 12-cup Bundt pan and increase the baking time to 1 hour.

BATTER

Vegetable oil cooking spray, for the pan

19 tablespoons (2 sticks plus 3 tablespoons) unsalted butter, softened

2¼ cups sugar

Zest of 2 lemons

2 tablespoons vanilla extract

5 large eggs

2⅓ cups all-purpose flour

2½ teaspoons baking powder

½ teaspoon salt

1¾ cups milk

¼ cup lemon juice

GLAZE

1¼ cups lemon juice

2½ cups sugar

1. Spray a 12-cup mini Bundt pan with vegetable oil cooking spray and set aside. Preheat the oven to 350°F.
2. In the large bowl of a stand mixer (or in a large bowl using a handheld mixer), cream together the butter, sugar, lemon zest, and vanilla.
3. Add the eggs one at a time, scraping down the sides of the bowl with a spatula between additions.
4. In a medium bowl, combine the flour, baking powder, and salt. Whisk to combine.
5. With the mixer on medium speed, add about one-third of the dry ingredients to the butter mixture. Mix until combined, then stop and scrape down the sides and bottom of the bowl with a spatula. With the mixer on medium speed again, add the milk and mix until combined, then stop and scrape down the sides and bottom

of the bowl with a spatula. Add another third of the dry ingredients, mix until combined, then scrape down with a spatula. Add the lemon juice, mix until combined, then scrape down with a spatula. Finally, add the remaining flour mixture and mix until combined.

6. Remove the bowl from the mixer and give the bowl a final scrape and stir with the spatula. Divide the batter among the cups in the Bundt pan.

7. Bake the cakes in the preheated oven until a toothpick inserted in the center of one comes out clean, about 20 minutes. Cool the cakes in the pan on rack for 5 minutes, then unmold and place directly on rack.

8. In a small bowl, combine the lemon juice and sugar for the glaze. Set the cooling rack on a jelly-roll pan or cookie sheet to catch drips. Dip the top of each cake into the glaze, then place on the rack to cool completely.

UKRAINIAN POPPY SEED CAKE

Makes two 9 × 5 × 3-inch loaf cakes; about 24 slices

This cake is very popular at Little Veselka, our outdoor kiosk, where we sell it by the slice, and it is frequently requested when we cater parties or donate food for events in the East Village. It's nice and moist, so you can slice it in advance and arrange the slices on a tray, and they'll still taste great at party time.

28 tablespoons (3 sticks plus 4 tablespoons) unsalted butter, softened, plus butter for pans

2½ cups sugar

2 teaspoons vanilla extract

Zest of 2 lemons

6 large eggs

4 cups all-purpose flour

½ teaspoon salt

1½ teaspoons baking powder

1 cup poppy seeds

2 cups milk

1. Butter two 9×5×3-inch loaf pans and set aside. Preheat the oven to 350°F.

2. In the large bowl of a stand mixer (or in a large bowl using a handheld mixer), cream together the butter, sugar, vanilla, and lemon zest until light and fluffy, about 3 minutes.

3. Add 2 of the eggs to the mixture and blend until combined. Stop and scrape down the sides of the bowl with a spatula. Add another 2 eggs and blend until combined. Stop and scrape down the sides of the bowl with a spatula. Add the remaining 2 eggs and blend until combined. Stop and scrape down the sides of the bowl with a spatula.

4. In a medium bowl, whisk together the flour, salt, baking powder, and poppy seeds.

5. Add about one-third of the flour mixture to the butter mixture and beat until combined, then add about one-third of the milk and beat until combined. Continue to alternate, adding about one-third of the total and beating smooth between additions, until the flour mixture and milk have been incorporated.

6. Pour the batter into the prepared loaf pans and bake the cakes for 15 minutes in the preheated oven. Reduce the oven temperature to 325°F and bake an addi-

tional 10 minutes, then reduce the temperature to 300°F. (Keep a close eye on the cakes and if they are beginning to brown too rapidly, reduce the heat sooner.) Bake until cakes are lightly browned and a toothpick or tester inserted in the center of one comes out dry, about 1 to 1½ hours.

7. Cool the cakes on a rack, still in the pans. When cakes are cool, gently turn out of the pans.

CARROT CAKE

Makes one 8-inch layer cake; about 12 servings

I don't know who the first person was to realize that shredded carrots would add moisture and heft to cake, but I thank her. Redolent of spices and not too sweet, this is one of the best versions of carrot cake I've ever tasted. This recipe makes a lot of frosting—enough for a really thick layer on top of your cake. If you prefer a carrot cake with less frosting, simply cut the frosting recipe in half.

CAKE

2 cups all-purpose flour

1½ teaspoons baking soda

1½ teaspoons salt

2¼ cups sugar

¾ teaspoon grated nutmeg

¾ teaspoon ground ginger

1½ teaspoons ground cinnamon

4 cups grated carrots, about 8 medium
  carrots

5 large eggs

2 cups vegetable oil

FROSTING

32 tablespoons (4 sticks) unsalted butter,
  softened

1 pound cream cheese, softened

4 cups confectioners' sugar, sifted

1 teaspoon vanilla extract

1. Preheat the oven to 325°F. Butter two 8-inch round cake pans, line with circles of parchment paper, and set aside.

2. In a large bowl, whisk together the flour, baking soda, salt, sugar, nutmeg, ginger, and cinnamon until combined. Add the grated carrots and toss until combined with the dry ingredients.

3. In a medium bowl, beat together the eggs and oil. Pour the wet ingredients into the dry ingredients and stir until combined.

4. Pour the batter into the prepared pans and bake until a toothpick inserted in the center of the cakes comes out clean, about 45 minutes. Unmold onto racks to cool.

5. To make the frosting, place the butter and cream cheese in the bowl of an electric mixer and mix until blended. Add the sugar and mix on low speed until sugar is

incorporated (to avoid a sugar cloud), then mix on high speed for 1 minute. Add the vanilla and mix until incorporated.

6. To assemble the cake, peel the parchment off the two cake layers. Place one layer on a cardboard or cake plate. Spread about one-third of the frosting over the top of the cake, using a metal cake spatula. Place the second layer upside down over the frosting so that the smoother side is on top. Frost the top and sides of the cake with the remaining frosting.

UKRAINIAN APPLE CRUMB CAKE

Makes one 7 × 7-inch square cake; about 6 servings

This is the sort of homey dessert that's perfect with a cup of coffee or tea in the afternoon, and it's quite simple to prepare. You can also prepare this in an 8 × 8-inch pan if that's all you have, but the cake will be a little thinner, so keep an eye on it and be sure not to over-bake.

CRUST

1½ cups graham cracker crumbs

8 tablespoons (1 stick) unsalted butter, melted, plus butter for the pan

FILLING

3 medium Granny Smith apples, cored, peeled and cut into ¼-inch dice

¼ cup sugar

1 tablespoon all-purpose flour

2 teaspoons ground cinnamon

TOPPING

½ cup all-purpose flour

½ cup sugar

½ cup light or dark brown sugar, firmly packed

½ cup almond flour

8 tablespoons (1 stick) unsalted butter, cold, cut into small pieces

1. Preheat the oven to 350°F.

2. Butter a 7×7-inch square baking pan and set aside. To make the crust, in a small bowl combine the graham cracker crumbs and the melted butter. Spread and press evenly into the bottom of the prepared pan.

3. To make the filling, toss together the apples, sugar, flour, and cinnamon. Distribute evenly over the crust.

4. To make the topping, combine the ingredients in a small bowl. Use your hands to combine them until the mixture is evenly moistened and resembles small pebbles. Distribute evenly on top of the apples.

5. Bake in the preheated oven until the crust is golden brown, 25 to 30 minutes. Serve warm or at room temperature.

SOUR CREAM CHEESECAKE

Makes one 10-inch cheesecake; about 14 servings

Some of the desserts at Veselka are of the traditional Ukrainian variety. Others are typical American diner-style treats. This cheesecake came from the mother of Lisa Straub, our pastry chef. Lisa has been making this cheesecake for so long that when she sat down to write the recipe, she realized she didn't know any of the measurements—she just eyes it all when she makes cheesecake at the restaurant. Sour cream is usually sold in 16-ounce containers, which will give you just about the right amount for the 14 ounces you need in the cake and a little for spreading on top to decorate it.

Vegetable oil cooking spray, for the pan

2 pounds 6 ounces cream cheese, softened

1½ cups plus 1 tablespoon sugar

5 large eggs

14 ounces sour cream, plus more for finishing

3 tablespoons vanilla extract

3 cups graham cracker crumbs, plus more for finishing

16 tablespoons (2 sticks) unsalted butter, melted

1. Preheat the the oven to 300°F. Line a 10-inch springform pan with 3-inch-high sides with a circle of parchment paper. Spray the parchment paper and the sides of the pan with vegetable oil cooking spray. Wrap the bottom of the pan and halfway up the sides with aluminum foil. Set aside.

2. In the large bowl of a stand mixer (or in a large bowl using a handheld mixer), mix the cream cheese and sugar until combined.

3. Scrape down the sides of the bowl with a spatula and then add the eggs one at a time, mixing until combined and then stopping to scrape down the sides of the bowl between each addition. Add the 14 ounces sour cream and vanilla and mix until combined.

4. Place the graham cracker crumbs in a medium bowl. Add about half of the melted butter and stir until combined. Add the remaining butter, about 1 tablespoon at a time, until the graham cracker crumbs are moist and stick together if you grab some in your fist. (You may not use all of the butter.)

5. Press the graham cracker crumbs firmly and evenly into the prepared pan. Pour in the sour cream batter and bake the cheesecake in a water bath until the filling is set, about 1 hour and 20 minutes.

6. Turn the oven off, open the oven door slightly, and let the cheesecake cool in the oven.

7. When the cake has cooled, remove it and refrigerate overnight.

8. To remove the chilled cake from the pan, place the pan in a sink or large wide bowl filled with about 1 inch of hot water (don't fill it too full or the water will come over the sides and into the cake) for a few minutes before unlocking the springform.

9. To finish the cake, spread the remaining sour cream on top and pat graham cracker crumbs on the sides.

APPLE PIES

Makes 6 individual 5-inch pies

There's no use even pretending that apple pie is a Ukrainian invention, is there? At the restaurant, rather than making one big apple pie, we bake up dozens of individual-sized ones. Everyone loves getting his or her own miniature pie, and they're much easier to serve that way. If you'd rather make one large pie, this should make a 9- or 10-inch pie. Pie crust makes people nervous, but it shouldn't. The only thing to keep in mind is that the butter and the water must be very cold when you start, and it shouldn't be overmixed.

FILLING

2 pounds (about 4 large) Granny Smith apples, cored, peeled, and sliced

½ cup orange juice

⅓ cup plus 1 tablespoon granulated sugar

¼ cup brown sugar, firmly packed

6 tablespoons unsalted butter

1½ teaspoons ground cinnamon

1½ teaspoons freshly grated nutmeg

½ cup apple cider

¼ cup cornstarch

CRUST

4 cups all-purpose flour

3 tablespoons sugar

1¼ teaspoons salt

4 sticks *very cold* unsalted butter, cut into cubes, plus more for buttering the pans

1¼ cups ice water

Egg wash: 1 large egg, lightly beaten

1. To make the filling, place the peeled and sliced apples in a large bowl and set aside.
2. In a medium saucepan, combine the orange juice, granulated sugar, brown sugar, butter, cinnamon, and nutmeg. Bring to a boil.
3. In a small bowl, whisk together the apple cider and cornstarch. When the orange juice mixture comes to a boil, pour in the apple cider mixture and cook over medium heat, whisking constantly, until the mixture thickens, 1 to 2 minutes.
4. Set the thickened mixture aside to cool for about 10 minutes. Whisk it again to loosen it, and pour it over the sliced apples. Stir to combine and set aside until completely cooled.

5. Meanwhile, butter six individual 5-inch pie pans (the disposable aluminum ones are fine) and set aside.

6. To make the dough, place the flour, 2½ tablespoons sugar, and salt in a medium bowl and stir to combine. Cut in the butter using a pastry blender or two knives until the mixture resembles coarse meal. Do not overwork—you want little pebbles of butter to remain. Sprinkle the water over the flour and butter mixture and stir with a fork just until the dough forms a ball. Again, do not overwork the dough. (Alternatively, make the dough in a food processor fitted with the metal blade: Pulse half the flour, half the sugar, and half the salt until combined. Add half the butter and pulse until mixture resembles coarse meal. With the machine running, sprinkle in ice water, 1 tablespoon at a time, just until the dough starts to form a ball. Repeat the process with the remaining flour, sugar, salt, and butter.)

7. Wrap the dough in plastic and chill the dough for 30 minutes to 1 hour.

8. On a lightly floured surface, form the dough into a rectangle about 1½ inches thick. Cut the rectangle into 12 equal pieces.

9. Using a well-floured rolling pin, roll out 6 of the pieces of dough into circles about ¾ inch larger than the diameter of the tart pans you are using. Place one in each of the prepared pans and press to fit.

10. Distribute the filling among the individual crusts.

11. Roll out the remaining 6 pieces of dough to circles that are about ¾-inch larger than the diameter of your pans. Top each individual pie with a circle of dough. Crimp the edges to seal the top and bottom crust. Refrigerate the pies for 1 hour before baking to prevent shrinkage.

12. Preheat the oven to 350°F. Brush the top crusts with the egg wash, sprinkle the remaining ½ tablespoon of sugar over the egg wash, and pierce the top crust of each pie with a paring knife to make a vent hole. Arrange the pies on jelly-roll pans so you can slide them into the oven easily. Bake the pies in the preheated oven until crust is dark golden brown, about 30 minutes.

CHERRY CRUMB PIES

Makes 8 individual 5-inch pies

We make our cherry pies with pitted cherries that are frozen with juice. These can be difficult to find, but they are well worth the effort. If you can't find them, you can substitute frozen or canned cherries and some cherry juice concentrate for them, but don't make the mistake of using gloppy canned cherry pie filling—it's way too sweet. This recipe can be used to make a single 10-inch pie, though the cooking time will be a little longer.

FILLING

½ cup cornstarch

3 pounds frozen pitted cherries in juice, thawed, juice reserved

3 cups sugar

CRUST

16 tablespoons (2 sticks) unsalted butter, plus more for buttering pans

1 cup sugar

1 tablespoon vanilla extract

1 large egg

2¾ cups all-purpose flour

STREUSEL TOPPING

1 cup brown sugar, firmly packed

2½ cups cake flour

¼ cup rolled oats

¾ teaspoon cinnamon

1 teaspoon baking powder

17 tablespoons (2 sticks plus 1 tablespoon) very cold unsalted butter, cubed

1. To make the filling, mix the cornstarch with 1 cup of cherry juice and set aside.

2. Combine the cherries, remaining juice, and sugar in a medium saucepan and bring to a boil.

3. Stir in the cornstarch mixture and return to a boil. Boil until the mixture begins to thicken, about 5 minutes. Remove the filling from the heat and pour into a bowl to cool.

4. Meanwhile, butter 8 individual 5-inch pie pans (the disposable aluminum ones are fine) and set aside.

5. To make the pie crust, in the bowl of a stand mixer (or in a large bowl using a handheld mixer), cream together the butter, sugar, and vanilla until light and fluffy, about 3 minutes. Add the egg. Blend until combined, then scrape down the sides of the bowl with a spatula. Add the flour and mix until combined. (Alternatively, to make the dough in a food processor fitted with a metal blade, combine the flour and sugar and pulse until combined. Add the egg, the vanilla, and then the butter, 1 tablespoon at a time, and process until the dough begins to come together in a ball.)

6. Wrap the dough in plastic wrap and refrigerate for at least 30 minutes.

7. While the dough is chilling, prepare the streusel topping. Combine the dry ingredients in a small bowl. Cut in the butter, using a pastry cutter or two knives, just until crumbly. Refrigerate until ready to use.

8. Preheat the oven to 350°F.

9. Form the dough into a rectangle about 1½ inches thick. Cut the rectangle into 8 equal pieces.

10. Roll out each of the 8 pieces of dough into a circle about ¾ inch larger than the diameter of the pans you are using. Place one in each of the prepared pans and press to fit.

11. Scoop the cooled cherry filling into unbaked shells. Sprinkle streusel topping over cherry filling.

12. Arrange the pies on jelly-roll pans so you can slide them into the oven easily. Bake in the preheated oven until the topping is a dark golden brown, 30 to 45 minutes.

Veselka's Famous Borscht (page 12)

Fried Pierogi (page 42)

Raspberry Blintzes (page 50)

Beet Salad (page 90)

Ukrainian Poppy Seed Cake (page 138) and Baked Chocolate Custard (page 130)

Triple Chocolate Mousse Tart (page 155)

Cheeseburger (page 198)

Blueberry Pancakes (page 218)

BLUEBERRY TARTS

Makes 10 individual 4½-inch tarts

Blueberries are delicious eaten out of hand, but they're even better—more intense and juicy—once they've been baked. These tarts are always a big hit with guests. The layer of frangipane (a kind of sweet almond cream) under the fruit is a lovely surprise. You can also make one large blueberry tart in a flat-bottomed, 10-inch tart pan with a removable rim. The only issue is that the crust tends to crack when you cut a larger tart, which looks messy. You can also make these in disposable aluminum pie tins if you don't have individual tart pans—they won't be quite as pretty, but they'll taste just as good.

CRUST

18 tablespoons (2 sticks plus 2 tablespoons) unsalted butter, plus more for buttering pans

1¼ cups sugar

1 tablespoon vanilla extract

1 large egg

3 cups all-purpose flour

FILLING

7 ounces almond paste

8 tablespoons (1 stick) unsalted butter

¼ teaspoon salt

⅔ cup plus 1 teaspoon sugar

3 large eggs

½ cup all-purpose flour

1½ cups blueberries

1 teaspoon ground cinnamon

¼ cup apricot preserves

1. Preheat the oven to 350°F. Butter 10 individual 4½-inch flat-bottomed tart pans and set aside.

2. To make the tart crust, in the large bowl of a stand mixer (or in a large bowl using a handheld mixer), cream together the butter, sugar, and vanilla until light and fluffy, about 3 minutes.

3. Add the egg and blend until combined, then scrape down the sides of the bowl with a spatula. Add the flour and mix until combined. Scrape down the sides of the bowl with a spatula again.

4. Wrap the dough in plastic wrap and refrigerate for at least 30 minutes.

5. While the dough is chilling, prepare the frangipane: In the large bowl of a stand mixer (or in a large bowl using a handheld mixer), cream together the almond paste, butter, salt, and ⅔ cup sugar until light and fluffy.

6. Add the eggs one at a time, beating smooth between additions, and then stopping and scraping down the sides of the bowl. When all the eggs have been incorporated, beat in the flour.

7. When you are ready to assemble the tarts, form the dough into a rectangle about 1½ inches thick. Cut the rectangle into 10 equal pieces.

8. On a well-floured work surface, using a floured rolling pin, roll out each of the 10 pieces of dough into a circle about ¾ inch larger than the diameter of the pans you are using. Place one in each of the prepared pans and press to fit.

9. Pour the frangipane into the tart shells and use a spatula to spread it evenly. The frangipane should be level with the top of the crust; you may have a small amount left over.

10. Arrange the blueberries in a single layer on top of the frangipane. Sprinkle on the cinnamon and the remaining 1 teaspoon of sugar. (It is useful to set the individual pans on one or two jelly-roll pans—this makes it easier to move them in and out of the oven.) Bake the tarts in the preheated oven until golden, 30 to 45 minutes.

11. Set the tarts on a rack to cool. Once the tarts have cooled, warm the apricot preserves in a small saucepan over low heat until liquid. (You may need to add 1 or 2 teaspoons of water.) Strain the preserves and brush onto the tarts to glaze them. Unmold the tarts and serve at room temperature.

BANANA CREAM PIES

Makes 8 individual 5-inch pies

I think these individual pies taste like delicious, sweet clouds. I can't get enough of the combination of whipped cream, bananas, and vanilla pastry cream. Both the crust and the pastry cream need to cook and cool before you can use them, so start these well in advance of when you want to serve them. This crust and pastry cream will make enough for a single 10-inch pie as well, though you may not need all of the banana slices to cover the surface, depending on the size of the bananas.

PASTRY CREAM

3¾ cups whole milk

¾ cup sugar

5 large egg yolks

¾ cup cornstarch

2 tablespoons all-purpose flour

2 tablespoons unsalted butter

3 tablespoons vanilla extract

FILLING

2 cups heavy cream

4 tablespoons sugar

6 ripe (but not mushy) bananas

2 tablespoons plus 2 teaspoons graham
  cracker crumbs

CRUST

16 tablespoons (2 sticks) unsalted butter,
  plus more for buttering the pans

1 cup sugar

1 tablespoon vanilla extract

1 large egg

2¾ cups all-purpose flour

1. To make the pastry cream, place 3½ cups of the milk and the sugar in a large saucepan and slowly bring to a boil. In a small bowl, mix together the egg yolks, cornstarch, flour, and remaining ¼ cup milk. Whisk thoroughly to avoid any lumps. When the milk begins to boil, ladle about 1 cup of the hot milk mixture into the egg yolk mixture and whisk vigorously. Return the milk to a boil and

pour the tempered egg yolk mixture slowly into the milk, whisking constantly. Keep whisking vigorously and bring the pastry cream to a boil again.

2. When the pastry cream boils a second time, remove the pan from the heat and whisk in the butter until completely melted and incorporated, then whisk in the vanilla. (It is helpful to use both a whisk and a spatula when mixing the pastry cream for the second boil. Whisk the mixture, and then scrape the bottom of the pot with the spatula, then whisk. This keeps it from scorching.)

3. If the cream looks lumpy, strain it through a fine-mesh sieve. (If you have whisked vigorously, this won't be necessary.) Transfer to a clean bowl and place a piece of plastic wrap or parchment paper on top so that it is directly touching the surface of the cream. Refrigerate the pastry cream for at least 8 hours before using.

4. To make the crusts, butter 8 individual 5-inch pie pans (the disposable aluminum ones are fine) and set aside.

5. In the large bowl of a stand mixer (or in a large bowl using a handheld mixer), cream together the butter, sugar, and vanilla until light and fluffy, about 3 minutes.

6. Add the egg. Blend until combined, then scrape down the sides of the bowl with a spatula. Add the flour and mix until combined.

7. Wrap the dough in plastic wrap and refrigerate for at least 30 minutes. Preheat the oven to 350°F.

8. Form the dough into a rectangle about 1½ inches thick. Cut the rectangle into 8 equal pieces.

9. On a well-floured work surface, using a floured rolling pin, roll out each of the 8 pieces of dough into a circle about ¾ inch larger than the diameter of the pans you are using. Place one in each of the prepared pans and press to fit. (It's convenient to arrange these on jelly-roll pans so you can slide them into the oven easily.) Poke each pie shell with a fork a couple times, then bake in the preheated oven until golden and crisp, 15 to 20 minutes. Set tart shells aside to cool.

10. To assemble the pies, whip the cream with the sugar until firm peaks form. Fill the cooled shells with pastry cream. Slice the bananas and cover the pastry cream with banana slices. Pipe whipped cream onto the pies with a pastry bag fitted with a star tip. Sprinkle 1 teaspoon graham cracker crumbs over each pie. Refrigerate the pies until serving time.

PEANUT BUTTER PIES

Makes 8 individual 5-inch pies

Peanut butter desserts can sometimes seem unsophisticated, but this one is fit for company. The cream cheese filling is actually a mousse, not some sticky kids' confection, and the chocolate crust gives it another flavor dimension. You can also use these amounts to make one 10-inch pie. At the restaurant, we often top these with chocolate shavings.

CRUST

16 tablespoons (2 sticks) unsalted butter, chilled, plus more for buttering pans

1 cup sugar

1 teaspoon vanilla extract

1 large egg

2 cups all-purpose flour

⅔ cup unsweetened cocoa powder, preferably Valrhona

FILLING

1½ cups peanut butter

12 ounces cream cheese, softened

12 tablespoons (1½ sticks) unsalted butter, softened

1½ cups plus 3 tablespoons sugar

1 tablespoon vanilla extract

1½ cups heavy cream

1. To make the crusts, butter 8 individual 5-inch pie pans (the disposable aluminum ones are fine) and set aside.

2. In the large bowl of a stand mixer (or in a large bowl using a handheld mixer), cream together the butter, sugar, and vanilla until light and fluffy, about 3 minutes.

3. Add the egg. Blend until combined, then scrape down the sides of the bowl with a spatula. Add the flour and cocoa powder and mix until combined.

4. Wrap the dough in plastic wrap and refrigerate for at least 30 minutes. Preheat the oven to 350°F.

5. Form the dough into a rectangle about 1½ inches thick. Cut the rectangle into 8 equal pieces.

6. On a well-floured work surface, using a floured rolling pin, roll out each of the 8 pieces of dough into a circle about ¾ inch larger than the diameter of the pans you are using. Place one in each of the prepared pans and press to fit. (It's convenient to

arrange these on jelly-roll pans so you can slide them into the oven easily.) Poke each pie crust with a fork a couple times, then bake in the preheated oven until crisp, about 15 minutes. Set the crusts aside to cool.

7. To make the filling, combine the peanut butter, cream cheese, butter, vanilla, and 1½ cups sugar in the bowl of an electric mixer and beat until very light and fluffy, about 5 minutes, stopping to scrape down the sides of the bowl occasionally.

8. In a clean bowl, whip the heavy cream and the remaining 3 tablespoons sugar to soft peaks. Gently fold about half of the whipped cream into the peanut butter mixture, then fold in the remaining whipped cream.

9. Distribute the filling among the cooled shells and smooth the tops with a spatula. Store in the refrigerator, but remove and let sit at room temperature for about 20 minutes before serving.

TRIPLE CHOCOLATE MOUSSE TART

Serves 8 to 12

This is one of the fanciest, most complex desserts that we serve at Veselka. It's an extremely impressive looking tart, but if you break it down, the individual components are not that complicated. (You will, however, need a candy thermometer in order to cook sugar to the soft ball stage.) Finally, this dessert not only can *be made in advance, but it* must *be made in advance, as it needs to set in the freezer overnight—that means it's perfect for your next dinner party.*

CHOCOLATE CRUST

Vegetable oil cooking spray, for the pan

12 ounces semisweet chocolate

6 tablespoons unsalted butter

3 large eggs

¼ cup sugar

MOUSSE

4 ounces semisweet chocolate

4 ounces white chocolate

4 ounces milk chocolate

12 tablespoons (1½ sticks) unsalted butter

3 sheets gelatin (see Note)

1¼ cups sugar

7 large egg yolks

4½ cups heavy cream

1. Spray a 10-inch springform pan with vegetable spray and set aside. Preheat the oven to 350°F.

2. To make the crust, combine the chocolate and butter in a medium-size heatproof bowl and set the bowl on top of a pot of boiling water to create a double boiler. Heat until the chocolate and butter have melted, then set aside.

3. In another medium heat-proof bowl, combine the eggs and sugar, set over the same pot of boiling water and heat the eggs and sugar, whisking constantly, until all of the sugar has dissolved and the mixture reaches about 110°F.

4. With an electric mixer, beat the egg mixture on high speed until light and fluffy. Fold the egg mixture into the chocolate and butter. Pour into the prepared pan and bake for 10 minutes. The batter will rise up and than fall, creating a dense chocolate brownielike crust. Set aside to cool.

5. To make the mousse, in three separate medium bowls, melt each type of chocolate with 4 tablespoons of butter. (The microwave is best for this—do this at short intervals and be careful not to overheat.) In three additional different bowls, soak 1 sheet of gelatin in 2 cups ice cold water and set aside to soften.

6. In a medium nonreactive pot, combine the sugar with just enough water to create a mixture the consistency of wet sand (about ½ cup of water, but it may vary depending on the weather and other factors). Bring the sugar mixture to a boil and brush the sides of the pot with a clean pastry brush dipped in ice water. Whisk the sugar mixture until all of the sugar crystals have dissolved. Again brush the sides of the pot with ice water to remove any crystals. Cook the sugar mixture to the soft ball stage (240°F). Separate the eggs and have the yolks ready beforehand, but be sure to cover the yolks—if they are left uncovered, a thin skin will form, and when you add the sugar the mixture will look unpleasantly lumpy.

7. When the sugar is cooked, place the egg yolks in the bowl of an electric mixer, then slowly pour in a little of the hot sugar while whipping on medium speed. (Be very careful not to burn yourself.) When yolks are warm, add a slow and steady stream of cooked sugar into the bowl while mixing constantly. When all of the sugar is incorporated, mix on high speed until the mixture has cooled and thickened.

8. Whip the cream to soft peaks and set aside.

9. Remove 1 sheet of gelatin from water and melt in the microwave for 10 seconds. Stir the gelatin into one of the chocolate and butter mixtures. Mix in about one-third of the yolk mixture until completely incorporated. Fold in about one-third of the whipped cream. Repeat with remaining two types of chocolate.

10. Randomly scoop each of the mousses into the prepared crust until the pan is filled. (This may look messy when you're doing it, but when you cut the tart it will have a lovely marbled look from the side.) Smooth the top of the tart with a spatula. Wrap the pan tightly in plastic wrap, and place in the freezer overnight until the mousse is very firm. (You may end up with a little extra mousse, which can be served unfrozen in a small bowl or dessert glass, or just eaten.)

11. Remove the tart from the springform pan while still very cold. Refrigerate until serving.

Note: Sheets of gelatin can be difficult to find. If you don't have any on hand, in step 5, separate 3 teaspoons of powdered gelatin (such as Knox) among 3 small microwave-safe bowls and dissolve in about 3 tablespoons of water each. In step 9, microwave each bowl of gelatin for 10 seconds to loosen, and continue with the recipe. To clean the pot you used to cook the sugar, fill it with water and return to a boil. Any hardened sugar will wipe away easily.

PEANUT BUTTER DOGGIE BISCUITS

Makes thirty-two 3-inch bone-shaped biscuits

We are big animal lovers at Veselka. I have a cat and a dog, and our pastry chef, Lisa Straub, has two dogs. Additionally, my wife, Sally, is a veterinarian with a practice right down the street. In warmer weather, we set out tables and chairs on the sidewalk, and we also leave big bowls of water outside for dogs to drink. These biscuits were Lisa's idea, and they were a great one—we often sell as many as two dozen in a single day! You can always tell when a dog has had a Veselka biscuit, too, because as the owner tries to pass by the corner of 9th Street and Second Avenue, the dog will pull hard on the leash, trying to get in the door. They're some of our most loyal customers. These biscuits stay good for several weeks if stored in an airtight container.

4 cups whole wheat flour	2 large eggs
8 ounces peanut butter	¾ cup oat bran
¼ cup vegetable oil	Pinch salt

1. Preheat the oven to 325°F. Line two large cookie sheets with parchment paper and set aside.
2. Mix all ingredients together in a large bowl. Add enough water to form a soft dough, about 1½ quarts.
3. Roll out dough to about ½ inch thick and cut out biscuits. We use a bone-shaped cookie cutter at Veselka, but you can make any shape you like, such as a person-shaped cookie cutter (the type usually used for gingerbread men). You can also simply cut the dough into squares or rectangles with a knife.
4. Transfer the biscuits to the prepared pans and bake in the preheated oven until very hard and dry, 45 minutes to 1 hour.
5. Allow to cool completely before transferring to an airtight container for long-term storage.

6

CHRISTMAS EVE:
A SPECIAL UKRAINIAN TRADITION

Kutya

Pickled Herring

Fish in Aspic

Gefilte Fish

Christmas Borscht

Vushka ("Little Ear" Dumplings)

Sauerkraut with Peas

Kasha Holubtsi (Stuffed Cabbage)

Simmered Mushrooms

Uzvar (Dried Fruit Compote)

CHRISTMAS IS MORE than a mere one-day holiday in Ukraine—it's an entire holiday season, a religious time that stretches from Christmas Eve until the Epiphany on January 20. The culinary highlight of that period is a meatless and dairy-free twelve-course feast on Christmas Eve. Interestingly, in Ukraine, Christmas was celebrated according to the Julian calendar, on the seventh of January, so Christmas Eve was January 6. After Ukrainian immigrants arrived in North America, most "adjusted" to the local Gregorian calendar. (See page 169 for more about Ukrainian Christmas Eve traditions.)

When I met my first wife in the 1960s and was welcomed into her large Ukrainian family—including her parents, the original owners of Veselka—all these traditions were new to me. I remember Christmas Eve dinner those early years could be a little overwhelming; there were many guests, and lots of food. The menu included all the dishes in this chapter, plus Potato Pierogi (page 40) made without farmer's cheese and with dairy-free dough, Sauerkraut and Mushroom Pierogi (page 44) made with dairy-free dough, and Mushroom Stuffed Cabbage (page 53), made with vegetable stock and vegetable oil. The meal went on for hours.

Like most American families, my own family celebrated holidays with a big meal—a turkey on Thanksgiving, a roast on Christmas—but what impressed me at the Darmochwal home was that they followed so many traditions. There were special toasts and special dishes, all eaten in a certain order. I loved seeing the extended family gathered like that—there was a great warmth to the occasion.

The Darmochwals had reason to celebrate, too. They had been lucky to have

Here I'm sharing a smile with some of Veselka's staff at our 1990 Christmas party. Christmas is always a special time at the restaurant. *(Sally Haddock)*

gotten out from under the thumb of the Soviets and fled to the West. After spending the immediate post-war years in a camp for displaced persons in Germany, they immigrated to the United States in 1949. They maintained traditions as a way of remembering their native land and their families and friends behind the Iron Curtain. A decade or two later, they were still celebrating Christmas with special gusto, as if to make up for lost time.

Today, my former brother-in-law Mykola Darmochwal and his wife, Zoriana Haftkowycz, keep these family traditions alive and host a big Christmas Eve dinner every year, and they still include me among the thirty or so guests. These days, I fit right in.

KUTYA

Serves 6 to 8

Not all Ukrainians eat the same menu on Christmas Eve, since there are some regional variations, but they do all eat kutya, a wheat dish that dates back to pagan times. Kutya bookends the meal: It is traditionally the first thing eaten, but since it is sweet, it makes another appearance as dessert. If you can't find wheat berries, barley makes an acceptable substitute and cooks more quickly.

1 cup wheat berries	1 cup honey
½ cup walnuts	½ cup canned poppy seed filling

1. The night before the day you wish to cook the kutya, place the wheat berries in a sieve and rinse well. Then place the rinsed wheat berries in a large bowl and add 3 cups water. Cover and set aside to soak at room temperature overnight.

2. The next morning, pour the wheat berries and their soaking water into a large pot. Bring to a boil, then reduce the heat to medium-low, and simmer until the wheat berries are tender, about 2 hours. Add more water in small amounts, if necessary, to keep the wheat berries submerged. When the wheat berries are tender and the majority of the kernels have burst, remove from the heat and set aside to cool.

3. While the wheat berries are cooking, chop the walnuts coarsely and toast in a small pan. Set aside to cool.

4. In a large bowl, combine the wheat berries with the honey. Stir to combine. Stir in the poppy seed filling and refrigerate to cool completely.

7. Serve the kutya in individual glasses with the toasted walnuts sprinkled on top.

PICKLED HERRING

Serves 8

Tart pickled herring is a great appetizer any day of the year, but it's particularly welcome as part of a rich Christmas Eve dinner. This kind of herring is widely available at New York City's many "appetizing stores," but it is relatively simple to make at home. The only difficult part may be finding salt-preserved herring. Your best bet is an Eastern European or Scandinavian ethnic specialty store (or see Resources on page 248). If you can't find salt-preserved herring, you can substitute canned (unsmoked) herring fillets, which allows you to skip the soaking and skinning and boning. Just arrange the fillets in a dish and pour the marinade over them. They won't have the same chewy texture as the salt-preserved fish, but they will be delicious nevertheless.

4 salt-preserved herring

½ cup white vinegar

6 whole black peppercorns

1 bay leaf

2 whole cloves

2 whole allspice berries

1 large onion, thinly sliced

1 tablespoon vegetable oil

1. Wash the herring under cold running water. Soak in cold water for at least 3 hours and preferably overnight, changing the water a couple of times.
2. Meanwhile, combine the vinegar, peppercorns, bay leaf, cloves, allspice, and ½ cup water in a medium saucepan. Bring to a boil, then set aside to cool.
3. Skin and fillet the herring. Discard the skin and bones and rinse the fillets under cold running water. Cut each fillet into 3 pieces.
4. In a glass container with a tight-fitting lid, arrange the herring and the onion slices in alternating layers.
5. Stir the vegetable oil into the cooled vinegar mixture, then pour the vinegar mixture over the herring and onions. Cover the container and refrigerate at least 24 hours before serving.

FISH IN ASPIC

Serves 6

Aspic is a savory gelatin concoction, and if that gives you visions of your mother's Jell-O salad, think again. A whole cooked fish robed in clear aspic is an impressive and elegant dish. You will need an aspic mold large enough to hold the fish—traditionally these are oval in shape. A 13×9-inch pan will also work.

1 whole white fish such as pike, 2½ to
  3 pounds, scaled and gutted

1 medium onion, peeled and roughly
  chopped

1 medium carrot, roughly chopped

1 celery stalk, roughly chopped

4 whole black peppercorns

1½ teaspoons salt

1 tablespoon gelatin

Fresh parsley sprigs, for garnish

Lemon slices, for garnish

1. To poach the fish, place the fish, onion, carrot, celery, peppercorns, and salt in a large pot with a tight-fitting lid. (A fish-poacher is perfect for this, but any pot large enough to hold the whole fish will do.) Add 4 cups water (if that doesn't cover the fish, add a little more). Bring to a boil, then reduce the heat and cook, covered, at a gentle simmer until fish flesh is opaque, about 5 minutes, depending on thickness of fish.

2. With a slotted spatula or strainer, remove the fish without breaking it up and set aside.

3. Strain the cooking liquid from the fish and discard vegetables and peppercorns. Return the stock to the same pot and bring to a boil. Boil until reduced by about half. (Refrigerate the fish in the meantime.)

4. While the stock is boiling, dissolve the gelatin in ¼ cup cold water. Set aside.

5. When the stock has reduced, add the gelatin to the stock and stir to combine. Taste stock and adjust seasoning.

6. Pour about ¼ inch of the stock into the mold you wish to use for the aspic, then refrigerate until softly set, about 1 hour.

7. Remove the fish bones and skin and discard, leaving the fish intact as much as possible. The skin of the cooked fish should peel away and the bones should lift out fairly easily—much more easily than if the fish were uncooked. Arrange the fish on top of the softly set aspic. If the cooked fish does break apart a little as you work with it, just arrange any pieces neatly in the mold and continue—it will still look pretty and will taste fine. Pour over the remaining stock and gelatin mixture and refrigerate until completely firm, at least 6 hours.

8. Just before serving, unmold the fish onto a platter. Garnish with the parsley sprigs and lemon slices and serve cold.

GEFILTE FISH

Makes 12 to 14 fish balls; about 6 servings

Somewhat counterintuitively, Ukrainians eat gefilte fish, a Jewish specialty, on Christmas Eve. No doubt this tradition was inherited from Ukrainian Jews—it's even called "Jewish-style fish." Zoriana Haftkowycz, wife of Mykola Darmochwal, who is the son of Veselka's founder, uses three kinds of fish in her version: pike, whitefish, and carp.

Christian Ukrainian immigrants like Veselka's founder, Wolodymyr Darmochwal, had an interesting relationship with Jewish Ukrainian immigrants, who for the most part had left Ukraine a little earlier. While in Ukraine the Jews and Christians didn't mingle much, when Christian Ukrainians came to New York City and other large American cities in the 1940s and 1950s, they often settled in Jewish neighborhoods. After all, the Jewish immigrants living there were from Eastern Europe and had traditions similar to theirs.

Wolodymyr was very close friends with the late Abe Lebewohl (tragically killed in 1996), who founded New York's famous Second Avenue Deli one block from Veselka, at Second Avenue and 10th Street in 1954, the same year that Wolodymyr opened Veselka. They considered each other comrades rather than competition. Like Veselka, the Deli started small with only ten seats, but it grew into a landmark, and even today (when the Second Avenue Deli is located at 33rd Street and Lexington Avenue) our menus overlap: Both serve blintzes, potato pancakes, and even chicken soup (though Second Avenue Deli is famous for their matzoh ball soup, and we serve noodles in ours).

1 pound pike fillets, skinned	1 small parsnip, peeled
1 pound whitefish fillets, skinned	2 large eggs
1 pound carp fillets, skinned	1 cup bread crumbs
2 small onions, peeled	Salt
2 carrots, peeled	Freshly ground black pepper

1. In a food processor fitted with the metal blade, grind together the fillets, 1 onion, 1 carrot, and the parsnip. The mixture should form a dry paste.
2. Add 1 egg to the mixture and mix with your hands to combine. Add the second egg and again mix with your hands to combine.

3. Sprinkle in about one-fourth of the bread crumbs and mix to combine. Continue adding the bread crumbs in small amounts until the mixture forms a ball that holds together when you roll it between your palms. You may not need all of the bread crumbs. If the mixture feels too dry, add a little water. Season the mixture with salt and pepper.

4. Roll the fish mixture into balls about 3 inches in diameter and divide them between two pots large enough to hold them in a single layer. Slice the remaining carrot and the remaining onion and add to the pot with the fish balls. Add water just to cover.

5. Place the pots over high heat and bring to a boil, then reduce the heat and simmer, and partially cover with a lid left slightly askew. Poach the fish balls until they are cooked through, about 30 minutes, shaking the pots occasionally to make sure the fish balls don't stick to the bottom, and adding a little additional water if necessary, to keep the pots from drying out.

6. When the fish balls are cooked through, use a slotted spoon to remove them to a shallow bowl. Strain the poaching liquid and pour a little (you probably won't need all of it) over the fish balls to moisten. Refrigerate the fish balls until serving and serve cold or at room temperature.

Abe Lebewohl (left) owned the Second Avenue Deli one block from Veselka. *(Second Avenue Deli)* Wolodymyr Darmochwal (right) stands in front of Veselka, circa 1967. *(Mykola Darmochwal)*

A Ukrainian Christmas Eve

For Ukrainians, Christmas Eve is one of the most important religious holidays of the year. Today, in the United States, most Ukrainian-Americans have moved the traditions—the big meal and other rituals—from January 6 to December 24. But the traditions themselves live on. Ukrainian Catholics, from western Ukraine, have a lot of their own specific Christian traditions. (People from eastern Ukraine tend to be Orthodox.) Rather than a Christmas tree—seen as a johnny-come-lately among Ukrainians—Ukrainians decorate the table with hay to symbolize the manger where Jesus was born. A special tablecloth is laid over the hay, and in some areas heads of garlic are placed around the table to ward off evil. Tradition also calls for a centerpiece of bread and evergreen branches and usually candles. Before any food is eaten, the head of the household goes into the yard and invites any evil spirits in the vicinity to join the feast; this is meant to placate them for the rest of the year. The meal is also shared with animals—again, a reflection of the story of Jesus in the manger, where animals were the first creatures to lay eyes on him—so a little of each dish is mixed into their feed.

Once the first star has appeared in the sky, the head of household greets all the guests holding a sheaf of wheat called a *dydukh,* which means "grandfather" or "old man." After the opening greeting is over, the wheat is placed in a corner, where it will remain throughout the holiday season. Then the woman of the home cuts a loaf of bread and presents each guest with a bit of bread dipped in honey.

Kutya (page 163), a sweet porridge of poppy seeds and wheat berries, is the first course of the Christmas Eve meal, and it has its own special blessing. The other dishes may vary from region to region and from family to family, but they usually feature a fair amount of fish, stuffed cabbage, and several different types of pierogi. Dessert is a stewed fruit compote and often *pumpushky,* which are similar to jelly doughnuts and are filled with poppy seed or rose preserves. After the meal, diners usually go caroling and then attend midnight mass.

At Veselka, we've developed our own Christmas tradition. For the last few years, we've served our version of the Ukrainian Christmas Eve feast at Veselka. We do a prix fixe menu, and while it's not quite twelve courses, it's pretty close. The menu is available both on December 24 and on January 6, and it includes classics such as Christmas Borscht with Vushka (page 171), but we try to modernize the meal a little, too. For example, we replace traditional Gefilte Fish (page 167) with a simple smoked salmon appetizer. Both Ukrainians who were raised on these foods and are pleased to see their old friends and non-Ukrainians who are simply curious about the menu tend to order it. We also distribute a brief description of Ukrainian Christmas traditions.

In general, November and December are busy months at Veselka. People are out and about, doing their shopping and visiting family, and they tend to drop in not just for meals, but for mid-afternoon and late-night snacks as well. On Christmas Eve and Christmas day, Veselka really fills up, since a lot of other restaurants are closed. Brunch on Christmas Day is particularly crowded, with both people celebrating Christmas and people of other religions. After all, they've got to eat, too!

CHRISTMAS BORSCHT

Makes 8 cups; about 6 servings

A special meatless borscht is always served for the Ukrainian celebration of Christmas Eve. At the Darmochwal home—where Mykola, the son of the original owner of Veselka, presides over the dinner—the meal always includes this clear borscht with little Vushka dumplings (page 173) floating in it.

2 pounds beets	2 bay leaves
¾ cup white vinegar	5 whole allspice berries
1 carrot, diced	2 tablespoons sugar
1 stalk celery, diced	1 garlic clove, minced
1 leek, diced	1½ teaspoons freshly ground black pepper
1 small onion, diced	Salt
4 cups Chicken Stock (page 35)	

1. Trim and scrub the beets and chop them, preferably, in a food processor fitted with the metal blade.
2. In a medium pot, combine the chopped beets, 4 cups water, and the white vinegar. Bring to a boil, then reduce the heat and simmer, uncovered, until the beets are soft and the liquid is a bright deep pink, about 45 minutes. (You may want to place a pot lid slightly ajar over the pot to keep your stovetop from getting splashed.) Strain and set the juice aside. (You can use the beets to make Beet Salad, page 90.)
3. Meanwhile, in a stockpot, combine the carrot, celery, leek, onion, chicken stock, bay leaves, and allspice berries. Bring to a boil, reduce the heat, and simmer, uncovered, for 45 minutes. (You may want to place a pot lid slightly ajar over the pot to keep your stovetop from getting splashed.)
4. Strain out and discard the vegetables and aromatics and return the strained stock to the pot. Stir in the beet juice and simmer gently for 5 minutes over medium-low heat.

5. Add the sugar gradually, about 1 teaspoon at a time, stopping to taste between additions. You may not want to use all of it, depending on how sweet your beets were. Stir in the freshly ground black pepper and garlic. Season to taste with salt.

6. To serve, ladle the borscht into individual soup bowls and float a few cooked Vushka in each bowl.

VUSHKA

("LITTLE EAR" DUMPLINGS)

Makes 80 dumplings; enough for 10 to 12 servings of Christmas Borscht

We make Vushka at Veselka during the Christmas season and serve them in our Christmas borscht. They are so addictive that I and the rest of the staff make a solemn promise at the start of the season not to eat any—otherwise we wouldn't have any left to sell. Vushka are made with the same dough we use for pierogi, but made with water instead of milk, and the dough is rolled thinner and cut smaller.

FILLING

¼ cup dried porcini mushrooms

3 tablespoons vegetable oil

1 small onion, minced

4 cups roughly chopped button
   mushrooms

Salt

Freshly ground black pepper

DOUGH

1 large egg yolk

1 tablespoon vegetable oil

3¼ cups all-purpose flour

1. To make the filling, rehydrate the dried mushrooms: Place them in a small bowl and pour about ¼ cup boiling water over them to cover. Set aside until softened, about 10 minutes. Drain the porcini, reserving the liquid, and set both aside.

2. Heat the vegetable oil in a large sauté pan. Add the onion and cook over medium heat, stirring occasionally, until the onion is translucent but not browned, about 5 minutes.

3. Add the fresh mushrooms and cook until the mushrooms have given up all their water and are greatly reduced in size. Season to taste with salt and pepper.

4. In the bowl of a food processor fitted with the metal blade, combine the cooked fresh mushrooms and the rehydrated porcini mushrooms. Carefully spoon out the clear soaking liquid from the porcini mushrooms and add it to the food processor, leaving the silt undisturbed at the bottom of the bowl. (Alternatively, strain it through a clean coffee filter.) Pulse the mushroom mixture three or four times until it is finely ground but not a paste—it should retain some chunks of mushroom and should not be runny or soupy. Set the filling aside while you make the dough.

5. To make the dough, in a measuring cup with a lip, combine the egg yolk, oil, and 1½ cups lukewarm water. Whisk with a fork for 1 minute. Place the flour in a large bowl. Make a well in the center and pour in the wet ingredients, about one-third at a time, using your fingers or a fork to incorporate the wet ingredients between additions.

6. When you have added all the wet ingredients, use your hands to fold the dough together. If it seems too dry and crumbly, add water, a few tablespoons at a time. If it seems too sticky, add a little more flour, about 1 teaspoon at a time to avoid making it too dry.

7. Transfer the dough to a lightly floured board and knead for 3 minutes. Again, add very small amounts of flour if the dough is too sticky to knead. When the dough is smooth and thoroughly incorporated, form it into a ball, transfer it to a small bowl, cover with plastic wrap, and refrigerate for 45 minutes. Clean and dry your work surface. Set aside a floured jelly-roll pan, platter, or cutting board for the finished vushka.

8. Divide the dough into three sections. Place one section on a well-floured work surface and roll out very thin—until almost translucent—with a well-floured rolling pin.

9. Cut the rolled dough into 1½ × 1½-inch squares. Dot the center of each square with about ½ teaspoon of the mushroom filling.

10. Fold squares in half to form triangles, sealing the edges tightly. (If the dough seems to be drying, lightly moisten your fingertips with water to seal the edges.) Pinch the two opposing corners together to form the "little ear" shape. As you finish filling and sealing each dumpling, place it on the floured jelly-roll pan; do not stack. (If it's very humid when you're making these, you may want to sprinkle a little flour on top of the vushka as well.) Repeat with second half of dough and the remaining filling.

11. Cook the vushka in abundant salted water until they float, 2 to 4 minutes. Drain and serve in Christmas Borscht (page 171).

SAUERKRAUT WITH PEAS

Serves 8

This vegetable dish is made of items that could be stored throughout the winter: dried peas and sauerkraut. The result is hearty and satisfying—kind of a thicker version of split pea soup with the salty punch of sauerkraut.

1 cup dried split peas, picked over and
   rinsed

3 cups sauerkraut, drained

1 garlic clove, peeled and left whole

1 tablespoon vegetable oil

1 large onion, diced

2 tablespoons all-purpose flour

Salt

Freshly ground black pepper

1. Place the peas in a pot and add water to cover, about 3 cups. Bring to a boil, then reduce the heat, and simmer until tender, about 30 minutes.
2. Meanwhile, in a medium pot, combine the sauerkraut and garlic with 1 cup water. Bring to a boil, reduce the heat, and simmer, uncovered, for 15 minutes.
3. In a small pan, heat the vegetable oil. Add the onion and cook until just beginning to turn golden. Sprinkle the flour over the onion and continue cooking until lightly browned.
4. Stir the onion and flour mixture and the cooked dried peas into the simmering sauerkraut and cook, stirring frequently, until very thick, about 10 additional minutes. Remove and discard the garlic. Season the mixture to taste with salt (you may not need any, depending on the saltiness of the sauerkraut) and pepper. Serve hot.

KASHA HOLUBTSI

(STUFFED CABBAGE)

Makes 10 to 12 pieces; about 6 servings

Holubtsi, *or stuffed cabbage, is traditionally served on Christmas Eve, but—as with the rest of the meal—it cannot have any meat in it. Traditional choices are this cabbage filled with cooked kasha (buckwheat groats) and the Mushroom-Stuffed Cabbage on page 53. Even confirmed carnivores won't miss the meat in these.*

1 large head cabbage	1 medium onion, diced
4 cups Vegetable Stock (page 36)	4 tablespoons vegetable oil
2 cups whole kasha	2 teaspoons salt
1 large egg, lightly beaten	

1. At least one day before you want to make the stuffed cabbage, core the heads of cabbage. Place cabbage in a large plastic freezer bag and freeze.

2. To make the kasha, in a small pot, bring the stock to a boil. When it is boiling, heat a medium sauté pan with a tight-fitting lid over medium heat.

3. In a small bowl, combine the kasha and egg. Add the kasha mixture to the dry pan and cook, stirring constantly, until the egg has dried and the kasha kernels are separate, about 3 minutes.

4. Carefully pour the boiling stock into the pan, stir to combine, and cover. Simmer over low heat until all the liquid has been absorbed and the kasha is tender, about 10 minutes for whole kasha.

5. Meanwhile, in a small sauté pan, sauté the diced onion in the oil until lightly browned, about 7 minutes. When the kasha is cooked, stir in the sautéed onion and set aside. (The kasha can be made up to this point and then refrigerated for a day or two.)

6. When you are ready to stuff the cabbage, pull the cabbage out of the freezer. Fill a large bowl with warm water and place the cabbage in the water to defrost. When the leaves are pliable, peel them off the head and set aside, being careful not to tear them. If a few do tear, set those aside for the bottom of the pot.

7. Place 3 or 4 leaves (including any torn ones) in the bottom of a very large pot. On top of the leaves place a heat-resistant plate or overturned pie pan or flat-bottomed steamer basket that sits about 1 inch above the bottom of the pot.

8. Place one cabbage leaf on the work surface. Place about ½ cup of the kasha filling in the center of the leaf and fold it envelope style (see illustration on page 52) to enclose the filling. Turn the leaf over and place it seam-side down in the pot on top of the plate or pie pan or steamer basket. Repeat with remaining leaves and filling. As you fold each leaf, tuck it tightly up against the others in the pot in a single layer. They should be touching on all sides and wedged together very firmly. When you've made one layer of cabbage packets, continue with a second layer on top, and so on until you have used up all the leaves and filling.

9. Add enough water to fill the pot about 3 inches. Cover, and place over high heat for 1 to 2 minutes to build up some steam, then lower the heat and steam the cabbage until the leaves are tender, about 1½ hours. Keep an eye on the water in the bottom of the pot to be sure it doesn't dry out; add a little extra water as the cabbage cooks, if necessary.

SIMMERED MUSHROOMS

Serves 6

During the rest of the year this side dish would be made with some sour cream stirred in at the end—a thicker version of the mushroom sauce we serve on our stuffed cabbage (page 56)—but on Christmas Eve, dairy is out of the question. This is usually served alongside the stuffed cabbage on Christmas Eve, though at other times of the year it might simply accompany some plain boiled potatoes.

2 tablespoons vegetable oil

1 medium onion, diced

1 garlic clove, minced

1 pound button mushrooms, cleaned and
    sliced

2 tablespoons flour

1 cup Vegetable Stock (page 36)

Salt

Freshly ground black pepper

2 tablespoons chopped fresh dill

1. Heat the oil in a large pan. Add the onion and cook over medium heat, stirring occasionally, until translucent, about 5 minutes. Add the garlic.
2. Add the mushrooms and continue cooking over medium heat until the mushrooms have given up their liquid and cooked down, about 7 minutes.
3. Sprinkle the flour over the mushrooms and stir to combine. Pour in the stock. Bring to a boil, reduce the heat, and simmer, stirring frequently, until thickened, about 10 minutes.
5. Season to taste with salt and pepper. Transfer to a serving bowl, sprinkle with the chopped dill, and serve immediately.

UZVAR

(DRIED FRUIT COMPOTE)

Serves 8

Uzvar is a compote of dried fruit. It is served at the end of the Christmas Eve meal in tall drinking glasses and is meant to be very liquid—you drink it rather than eating it with a spoon. This recipe will work with almost any type of dried fruit, so feel free to use this as a guideline and not a set of hard-and-fast rules. In fact, a dried fruit compote is a great way to use up any odds and ends of dried fruit that are becoming a little too chewy with age. Compote keeps in the refrigerator for a week or two and is nice to have on hand at any time of the year—mixed with yogurt it makes a wonderful breakfast.

1 cup (about 8 ounces) dried apple slices

1 cup (about 8 ounces) dried pear halves

½ cup (about 4 ounces) pitted prunes

½ cup (about 4 ounces) raisins

1 lemon

1 cup honey

1 cinnamon stick

4 whole cloves

2 quarts apple cider

1. Cut the apple slices and pear halves in halves or quarters.
2. In a medium nonreactive pot, combine the apples, pears, prunes, and raisins.
3. With a vegetable peeler, remove the peel from the lemon (leaving behind any white pith) and add the peel to the pot. Juice the lemon and add the lemon juice to the pot as well.
4. Stir in the honey, cinnamon stick, cloves, and apple cider. The liquid should cover the contents of the pot by at least 1 inch. If it does not, add more cider or cold water.
5. Cover the pot with a lid, bring to a boil, then reduce the heat and simmer until the fruit is very tender but pieces are not falling apart, 15 to 20 minutes.
6. Remove and discard the lemon peel, cinnamon stick, and cloves. Taste and adjust sweetness by adding honey or lemon juice, if necessary. Serve warm.

7
SANDWICHES

Challah

Whole Wheat Bread

Fried Egg Sandwiches

The Andy Warhola (Pop Artist)

The Leon Trotsky (Revolutionary)

Tuna Melts

Hamburgers

   Cheeseburgers

   Bacon Cheeseburgers

Lamb Burgers

Buffalo Burgers

Turkey Burgers

Smoked Salmon on a Bagel with
   Tomato, Onion, and a Schmear

Fried Fish Sandwiches

The Rinat Akhmetov (Ukraine's
   Richest Man)

*The Viktor Pinchuk (Ukraine's
   Second Richest Man)*

The Milla Jovovich (Supermodel)

The Leonid Stadnik (The World's
   Tallest Man)

The Madame Alexander (Doll
   Manufacturer)

IN THE LAND OF THE SANDWICH, bread is king. Actually, any sandwich will only be as good as the quality of all its parts, but it seems to me that if you can't get your hands on good-quality bread, you ought to skip the sandwich completely. Matching the correct type of bread with the sandwich filling is important, too. And today, Americans' expectations about bread are higher than ever. There are artisanal bakeries popping up all over the country. Still, bread you make at home always tastes great. The bread recipes in this chapter require surprisingly little effort, and since each one makes two loaves, you can easily have homemade bread on hand at all times. Try them once and you may never buy sandwich bread again.

Sandwiches were some of the first "American" food served at Veselka. In the 1960s, when pierogi and borscht were still the big draw, Wolodymyr Darmochwal added tuna fish sandwiches, grilled cheese, egg salad sandwiches, hamburgers, and BLTs to the menu to attract some non-Ukrainian customers. Back then, as now, everything was made to order—I've never liked the idea of premade sandwiches wrapped in plastic and stacked up near the register, though they would probably make the take-out process a little faster.

We hear all the time that our simpler sandwiches taste "just the way Mom made them," which I think is a tremendous compliment. Yes, everyone likes fancy food sometimes, but there's also great satisfaction to be found in eating something you loved as a child and finding that it still tastes the same. For most Americans, tuna sandwiches were a lunch staple.

We sell a lot of sandwiches at our Little Veselka kiosk in First Park, which is located at First Avenue and 1st Street, about ten blocks from the restaurant. The first time I saw that kiosk, I just fell in love with it. My son Jason and I put together a proposal for how we would run it and what kind of rent we would pay and went through an interview process with the city to get permission to take it over. We opened the kiosk in the summer of 2006.

The kiosk doesn't have an actual kitchen, of course, but it has a couple of panini presses for making hot sandwiches and we can grill kielbasa there. We serve a more limited menu there, but we serve lots and lots of sandwiches, most of them named for famous Ukrainians. There are chairs and tables in the park, and eating at Little Veselka is a bit like going on a picnic.

Most sandwiches at both Veselka and Little Veselka come with Coleslaw (page 93) and a pickle, too. Like high-quality bread, those seem to make everything taste better.

Our Little Veselka kiosk at 1st Street and First Avenue sells sandwiches named for famous Ukrainians. *(Sally Haddock)*

CHALLAH

Makes two 9-by-4-inch loaves; about 12 slices each

Challah is a soft, eggy bread similar to French brioche. While challah is originally Jewish, and slicing a loaf of challah on a Friday night is part of welcoming the Jewish Sabbath, you don't have to be Jewish to love it. We don't braid our challah, but instead make it into a Pullman loaf and use it for many of the sandwiches on Veselka's menu, and we make it in batches of twenty-three loaves at a time. Challah is delicious as is, especially when fresh, but it also makes wonderful toast. In fact, many of our customers order a couple slices of toasted challah with their soup. This bread freezes wonderfully, too. The easiest thing to do is to slice the loaf in advance, and then toast individual slices to defrost them.

2 envelopes active dry yeast (about 5 teaspoons)

½ cup sugar

2 large eggs

¼ cup vegetable oil

5 to 6 cups bread flour

1½ teaspoons salt

Vegetable oil cooking spray, for the bowl and pans

Egg wash: 1 large egg yolk whisked with 2 teaspoons water

1. In a large mixing bowl, combine the yeast, 1 cup warm water, and sugar. Let stand until the yeast blooms, about 5 minutes.
2. In a small bowl, whisk the eggs with the vegetable oil. Add the egg mixture to the yeast mixture, along with 5 cups of the bread flour and the salt. Mix the ingredients using a wooden spoon, an electric mixer fitted with the dough hook, or your hands until the dough comes together, adding the additional 1 cup of bread flour in small amounts, if needed.
3. Turn the dough out onto a floured work surface and knead until smooth and elastic, 8 to 10 minutes. The dough should be firm, but not dry.
4. Lightly spray a large bowl with cooking spray. Add the dough, turning to coat. Cover with plastic wrap and allow to rise in a warm, draft-free area until doubled in volume, about 1 hour.

5. Punch down the dough. Cover again with plastic wrap, and allow to rise for an additional 30 minutes.

6. Lightly spray two 9×4-inch loaf pans with cooking spray and dust them with flour, tapping out the excess. Divide the dough into two equal pieces and shape each piece of dough into a Pullman loaf (press each piece into a rectangle, then roll each rectangle into a log). Place the loaves in pans. Cover loosely with plastic wrap and allow to rise until almost doubled, about 30 minutes.

7. Preheat the oven to 375°F. Uncover the dough. Brush the tops of the loaves with egg wash. Bake in the preheated oven until the loaves are browned on the bottom and sound hollow when tapped, about 35 minutes. Allow the loaves to cool in the pans for 10 minutes, then remove and cool completely on a wire rack.

WHOLE WHEAT BREAD

Makes two 9-by-4-inch loaves; about 12 slices each

These days, we buy the whole wheat bread we use at Veselka. We go through so many loaves of it every day that making it ourselves became untenable a few years ago. But this is the recipe for the whole wheat bread we used to make at Veselka. It was very popular, and we still get a few requests every year for the recipe, so I wanted to include it here. Like the challah, this freezes nicely, especially if you slice it first. Be sure to let the bread cool completely before you cut it, even though freshly baked bread can be difficult to resist.

2 tablespoons molasses

2 envelopes active dry yeast (about 5 teaspoons)

¼ cup vegetable oil

2 cups whole wheat flour

3 to 4 cups bread flour

1½ teaspoons salt

Vegetable oil cooking spray, for the bowl and pans

1. In a large mixing bowl, combine the molasses, yeast, and 1½ cups warm water. Let stand until the yeast blooms, about 5 minutes.
2. Add the vegetable oil, whole wheat flour, 3 cups of the bread flour, and the salt to the yeast mixture. Mix the ingredients using a wooden spoon, an electric mixer, or your hands until the dough comes together, adding the additional 1 cup of bread flour in small amounts if needed.
3. Turn the dough out onto a floured work surface and knead until smooth and elastic, 8 to 10 minutes. The dough should be firm, but not dry.
4. Lightly spray a large bowl with cooking spray. Add the dough, turning to coat. Cover with plastic wrap and allow to rise in a warm, draft-free area until doubled in volume, about 1 hour.
5. Punch down the dough. Cover again with plastic wrap, and allow to rise for an additional 30 minutes.
6. Lightly spray two 9×4-inch loaf pans with cooking spray and dust with flour, tapping out the excess. Divide the dough into two equal pieces and shape each

piece into a loaf (press the dough into a rectangle, then roll each rectangle into a log). Place the loaves in pans. Cover with plastic wrap and allow to rise until almost doubled, about 30 minutes.

7. Preheat the oven to 350°F. Uncover the dough. Bake the loaves in the preheated oven until they are browned on the bottom and sound hollow when tapped, about 35 minutes. Allow the loaves to cool in the pans for 10 minutes, then remove and cool completely on a wire rack.

Two Brothers and a Bakery

These days, we bake our own challah at Veselka. We buy seeded buns for burgers from Amy's Bread (a contemporary New York City institution run by Amy Scherber). A Polish bakery, Solina, supplies us with seven-grain, whole wheat, and rye bread that's perfect for sandwiches because it's baked like a Pullman loaf. (Customers in this neighborhood, which has a long tradition of Jewish delis, are particularly picky about their rye bread.) But when I first started working at Veselka and for many years afterward, we bought our bread from a place called Ninth Street Bakery.

The name was actually a misnomer—nothing was ever baked at the store located at 350 East 9th Street, down the block from Veselka. Instead, it sold bread and other baked goods from a variety of bakeries in the area to both restaurants and retail customers. The place was a neighborhood legend, as were its proprietors, two brothers, Joe and Harry, who seemed to be at the store day and night. I sometimes imagined that they slept there, in the back room, an image encouraged by the frequent sight of Joe dozing in the store during the day, his head leaning against the bread slicer. In short, they were real characters, and like many in the neighborhood, I was fascinated by them. Eventually Veselka stopped buying bread from them, and then they were no longer behind the counter, though the store remains open to this day.

In 2007, a friend who also works in the neighborhood handed me a page torn from *The New York Times Book Review*: It was a rave review for a memoir titled *Dough*, written by Mort Zachter about his quirky uncles on his mother's side, Harry and Joe, who ran the Ninth Street Bakery. I rushed out to buy a copy and was stunned—as their nephew, their only descendant, had been—to learn that the two brothers, now both deceased, had actually been millionaires. One day I invited Mort—whose memoir is now available in paperback and who is as thoughtful and funny in person as he is in print—to Veselka, and we reminisced about Harry and Joe.

Tom: I felt like I had such an intimate relationship with your uncles, be-cause I called or went every day for bread. They were always there.

Mort: Joe was there from early in the morning when the deliveries came until midnight came around or they sold all the bread. They closed only on Passover, Rosh Hashanah, and Yom Kippur. The store was their social life, too. They never married. They never had kids. The bakery was their world. In later years there was a Ukrainian lady, Mary, who worked there, but they wouldn't let her work the register. That was only family.

Tom: There were so many rumors and a kind of mystique about that place. One rumor I heard was that Mary didn't get paid. People said, "She delivers the bread because she likes it." We'd feel sorry for Mary and give her a dollar.

Mort: The sad thing is, by the time I really wanted to know more, Uncle Joe was gone and Uncle Harry didn't remember.

Tom: What happened to the store?

Mort: They sold the store in 1986 for $12,000, payable over four years in installments. The store had never closed, except after Joe died and Harry got sick in the early 1980s. Finally, they sold it to a fellow who was Ortho-dox, and he closed it on Saturdays. Then he became ill, and they had a young Ukrainian fellow working there who was an immigrant and they sold it to him. He and his wife are still there now. They were very interested in how my uncles made so much money. I explained to them they never spent it and they just never stopped working. The new owners refurbished the store. I went in right after they finished, and everything was new and sparkling. There were counters and everything was behind glass. When my uncles were there everything was open. And they never posted prices.

They would check you out and decide what to charge you. Uncle Joe was a master at that. The new owners also opened up on Saturdays again.

Tom: When your uncles were there, Saturday was the busiest day. I never got to know your mom because I didn't go on Saturdays—it was too busy.

Mort: My mother got married in the 1950s and I was born in 1958. She had a master's degree in education and she worked as a teacher, but she still went to the store on Saturdays until they sold it in 1986. I remember her dragging me there when I was little. I was like a surrogate son to my uncles, and they wanted me to work there, but my mother refused to let me.

Tom: Joe was so funny and always happy to see me, and one reason I never went on Saturdays was that I didn't like going there and dealing with somebody else.

Mort: He had this caustic, wry sense of humor. He had these expressions, like "he's the boss and I'm the horse," because he would always be there working.

Tom: What are your memories of the neighborhood back then?

Mort: In the early 1960s, 9th Street was still paved with cobblestones. At the corner of 9th Street and First Avenue on the south side of the street there was a health food store. They sold juice, and eventually they were involved in the founding of Snapple. The block was mostly this mix of old world Ukrainian and very 1960s mod fashion places that were selling all kinds of *shmattes*.

Tom: I remember the block was much quieter then. There wasn't so much traffic. Kids could play stickball in the street and a car wouldn't go by. People sat on lawn chairs on the sidewalk in the evening or out on the fire escapes. Everybody knew everybody.

Mort: Yes, it was a working-class neighborhood back then. I learned how to ride a bicycle on this block. My uncles bought me the bicycle. They bought it at Stuyvesant Bicycle Shop, and they gave us a good price because they knew Uncle Harry. There was a wonderful hardware store for years and years. I think there's a Japanese restaurant there now. On Second Avenue there was a famous dairy restaurant, Ratner's, and Moishe's, which is still there, was my uncles' competition. It's very different now. There's a luxury hotel on the Bowery with imported 400-thread-count, Egyptian cotton bed sheets!

Tom: Things certainly have changed.

Mort: On one hand, it saddens me. But New York is ever-changing. The neighborhoods ebb and flow. Come back in 100 years—who knows what will be?

FRIED EGG SANDWICHES

Serves 4

A fried egg sandwich is one of life's great pleasures, and also something that's great to make when you feel as if you have no food in the house, since you probably always have a couple of eggs and a couple of slices of bread. I give instructions below for cooking the eggs over-easy as well, but really most of the joy to be found in this sandwich comes from the toast soaking up the uncooked yolk.

4 eggs	2 tablespoons butter
8 slices white or whole wheat sandwich	Salt
bread, toasted	Freshly ground black pepper

1. Set a medium skillet, preferably cast-iron, over medium heat and heat for 2 minutes. Crack the eggs into a medium bowl without breaking yolks. Place one piece of toast on each of four serving plates.
2. Add the butter to the skillet and allow it to melt.
3. When a few bubbles have formed in the melted butter, gently tilt the bowl and slide the eggs into the skillet. Season to taste with salt and pepper.
4. Cook for a few minutes until the edges of the whites begin to brown. Carefully tilt the pan and spoon up the melted butter from the side. Baste the eggs with the melted butter. Continue cooking, basting occasionally with the butter, until the whites are set, 2 to 3 minutes. (Alternatively, for over-easy eggs, flip the eggs with a metal spatula and cook about 2 minutes on each side.)
5. With the edge of a metal spatula, cut through the egg whites to divide the eggs. Place one egg on each slice of toast. Top with a second slice and serve immediately.

THE ANDY WARHOLA (POP ARTIST)

CLASSIC EGG SALAD ON CHALLAH

Serves 4

If Veselka were a famous person, it would be Andy Warhol: He's unmistakably associated with New York City, but his roots reached back to Ukraine, and he was a quirky artist, as are so many of our customers. Warhola *is the possessive form of the artist's last name.*

8 slices Challah (page 185) 1 cup Egg Salad (page 97)

¼ cup mayonnaise

1. Spread each slice of challah on one side with about ½ tablespoon of mayonnaise.

2. Spread about ¼ cup egg salad on each of 4 slices of bread.

3. Top with the remaining 4 slices of bread, mayonnaise-side down. Slice on the diagonal and serve immediately.

THE LEON TROTSKY (REVOLUTIONARY)

CLASSIC TUNA SANDWICH ON CHALLAH

Serves 4

I'm not really sure that Leon Trotsky loved a classic tuna sandwich, but who wouldn't? On soft, fresh challah, these are a real treat.

8 slices Challah (page 185)   1 cup Tuna Salad (page 96)
¼ cup mayonnaise

1. Spread each slice of challah on one side with about ½ tablespoon of mayonnaise.
2. Spread about ¼ cup tuna salad on each of 4 slices of bread.
3. Top with the remaining 4 slices of bread, mayonnaise-side down. Slice on the diagonal and serve immediately.

TUNA MELTS

Serves 4

The ideal tuna melt requires a few simple things: great tuna salad (check), tasty but not overpowering cheese (check), and crisp toast as a base (check).

1 tablespoon mayonnaise

4 slices rye or other bread, toasted

1 cup Tuna Salad (page 96)

4 slices Vermont cheddar or other cheese

1. Preheat the broiler.

2. Line a cookie sheet or jelly-roll pan with aluminum foil.

3. Spread a little of the mayonnaise on each slice of bread and place mayonnaise-side up on the pan.

4. Divide the tuna salad among the four slices of toast and press flat with the back of a fork, distributing it evenly over the toast.

5. Top each sandwich with a slice of cheese.

6. Broil until the cheese melts, about 2 minutes. Serve immediately.

HAMBURGERS

Serves 4

The hamburger is another example of a simple food that Veselka's customers insist just tastes better at the restaurant. We sell about 500 hamburgers in a typical week, which is a high number given how broad our menu is. Actually, it's not only customers who love Veselka's burgers: The local press has a soft spot for them, too. Our biggest journalist fan is probably Josh Ozersky, aka Mr. Cutlets, online food editor for New York *magazine and also the author of a book titled* Meat Me in Manhattan: A Carnivore's Guide to New York. *On more than one occasion, he has called Veselka's the best burger in town. We use brioche buns from Amy's Bread, which are sprinkled on both sides with sesame seeds. I think the crunch is part of what makes the Veselka burger—plain as it may be—special. Also, unlike a lot of diners, we char-broil our burgers rather than cooking them on a griddle. We don't serve lettuce or tomato on our burgers either—that way the meaty flavor really stands out.*

2 pounds ground chuck

Salt

Freshly ground black pepper

4 sesame hamburger buns, split

1. Prepare a gas or charcoal grill.
2. Place the meat in a medium bowl. Season to taste with salt and pepper and mix with your hands to combine.
3. Divide the meat into 4 equal portions (8 ounces each), and shape each portion into a thin patty about the same diameter as the buns you are using. The meat should be in a thin layer and should almost completely cover the bun.
4. Grill the burgers to desired doneness, turning once with a spatula. At Veselka, we prefer them rare or medium rare, which means cooking them only about 2 minutes per side because they are so thin.
5. Briefly toast the buns on the grill while the burgers are cooking.
6. Place the burgers on the buns and serve immediately.

Variations: For Cheeseburgers, in step 4, when you have already turned the burgers once, place a slice of American cheese or Vermont cheddar on top of each. We don't leave the burgers on the grill long with the cheese on top—the heat of the toasted bun continues to melt the cheese after you remove the hamburgers. To gild the lily completely and make Bacon Cheeseburgers, cook 8 strips of bacon in a cast-iron skillet on the stovetop until crispy, then place 2 strips on top of each of the cheeseburgers before topping them with the top halves of their buns.

LAMB BURGERS

Serves 4

Lamb makes for a richer burger and offers a subtle change from the usual beef burgers. For a Greek-style cheeseburger, we top these with feta cheese sometimes.

2 pounds ground lamb	Salt
1 small onion, minced	Freshly ground black pepper
1 garlic clove, minced	4 sesame hamburger buns, split

1. Prepare a gas or charcoal grill.
2. Place the meat in a medium bowl. Add the onion and garlic and season to taste with salt and pepper. Mix with your hands to combine.
3. Divide the meat into 4 equal portions (8 ounces each), and shape each portion into a patty about the same diameter as the buns you are using.
4. Grill the burgers to desired doneness, turning once with a spatula.
5. Briefly toast the buns on the grill while the burgers are cooking.
6. Place the burgers on the buns and serve immediately.

BUFFALO BURGERS

Serves 4

Buffalo is an up-and-coming meat. Like beef, it's rich in iron and protein, but it's relatively low in fat. Buffalo meat is also more and more commonly available in grocery stores and at traditional butchers, but if you can't find a store near you that sells it, check out Resources on page 246 for places you can order it online. The chipotle mayonnaise we serve on these burgers is delicious. You can alter the heat by adjusting the number of peppers you use. Chipotle peppers are simply smoked jalapeño peppers, and they are widely available packed in adobo sauce in 7-ounce cans.

¼ cup mayonnaise

1 chipotle pepper in adobo sauce or more to taste

2 pounds ground buffalo meat

Salt

Freshly ground black pepper

4 sesame hamburger buns, split

1. Heat a gas or charcoal grill.
2. In a food processor fitted with a metal blade, process the mayonnaise and chipotle pepper until smooth. Taste and adjust by puréeing in more peppers, if desired. Set aside.
2. Place the meat in a medium bowl. Season to taste with salt and pepper and mix with your hands to combine.
3. Divide the meat into 4 equal portions (8 ounces each), and shape each portion into a patty about ½ inch thick.
4. Grill the burgers to desired doneness, turning once with a spatula. At Veselka, we prefer them medium rare, which means cooking them 3 minutes per side.
5. Briefly toast the buns on the grill while the burgers are cooking.
6. Remove the buns to individual serving plates. Spread about 1 tablespoon chipotle mayonnaise on the top half of each bun. Place a cooked burger on the bottom half of each bun. Assemble and serve.

TURKEY BURGERS

Serves 6

Turkey Burgers have gotten increasingly popular over the years as customers have grown concerned about their consumption of red meat. Turkey can be a little more bland, though, than beef, so we up the flavor quotient with some garlic and onion and thyme.

2¼ pounds ground turkey

1 garlic clove, minced

½ large yellow onion, minced

2 teaspoons dried thyme

Salt

Freshly ground black pepper

6 sesame hamburger buns

6 lettuce leaves

1 medium tomato, sliced

1. Preheat the grill for about 30 minutes.
2. In a medium bowl, combine the turkey, garlic, onion, and thyme. Season to taste with salt and pepper. Mix by hand until thoroughly combined.
3. Divide the meat into 6 equal portions (6 ounces each) and shape each portion into a patty.
3. Grill the burgers until completely cooked, 10 to 12 minutes, turning 4 or 5 times.
4. Serve the burgers on the buns. Top each burger with a lettuce leaf and a couple slices of tomato. Assemble and serve.

SMOKED SALMON ON A BAGEL WITH TOMATO, ONION, AND A SCHMEAR

Serves 4

A New York City classic, there is no doubt that this tastes best when you're seated at the counter at Veselka with a cup of coffee and a Sunday New York Times. *At the restaurant, we use H&H bagels, Philadelphia cream cheese, and smoked salmon from Catsmo, a company that smokes imported salmon in the Catskills (see Resources on page 248 for more information). The best way to serve this at home is to set out a basket of sliced bagels (a true and good bagel does not need to be toasted), a platter of fish, a sliced onion, a sliced tomato, and a little tub of cream cheese and allow guests to serve themselves.*

4 plain bagels, halved

8 ounces cream cheese

1 small red onion, thinly sliced

1 medium tomato, stem end removed, thinly sliced

8 ounces thinly sliced Nova-style smoked salmon

1. Set each of the bagels on an individual serving plate.

2. Spread the cut side of the bottom half of each bagel with cream cheese.

3. Top the cream cheese with a slice or two of onion.

4. Top the onion with a slice or two of tomato.

5. Distribute the salmon over the top of the tomato. Top with the other half of the bagel and serve at room temperature.

FRIED FISH SANDWICHES

Serves 4

We make our fish fillet sandwiches with tilapia, though you could use any mild-flavored thin white fish. If you own one of those handy electric deep fryers, this is the time to pull it out and put it to good use. It makes the preparation much easier.

Vegetable oil, for frying

1¼ cups all-purpose flour

¾ cup beer

½ teaspoon salt

4 skinless tilapia fillets, about 2 pounds total

4 sesame hamburger buns, split

4 leaves lettuce

¼ cup tartar sauce

1. Fill a large, heavy pot with enough vegetable oil to come about 2 inches up the side. Place over high heat and heat until the oil registers 380°F on a thermometer. (A small cube of bread, dropped in the oil, should turn brown in under 1 minute.)

2. Meanwhile, spread ½ cup of the flour on a large plate. In a medium shallow bowl, whisk together the remaining ¾ cup flour, the beer, and the salt until very smooth. Add a small amount of additional beer or a little water if the batter seems too thick.

3. Pat the tilapia fillets dry. Dredge them first in the flour, and then in the beer batter. Use tongs to take them out of the beer batter, and transfer them to the hot fat.

4. Fry each fillet until golden, turning once with tongs, about 6 minutes.

5. Transfer the cooked fillets to paper towels to drain briefly, then place one fillet on each bun. Top with lettuce leaves and tartar sauce (or serve the sauce on the side) and serve immediately.

THE RINAT AKHMETOV (UKRAINE'S RICHEST MAN)
GRILLED VERMONT CHEDDAR ON CHALLAH

Makes 1 sandwich

It has become increasingly common for home cooks to make "grilled cheese sandwiches" by toasting the bread in a toaster oven and then melting the cheese on the toasted bread. While this doesn't taste bad, exactly, we still make grilled cheese sandwiches the old-fashioned way at Veselka: on a griddle with a little butter. A well-seasoned cast-iron pan is perfect for this. We use Cabot's Vermont cheddar and our own challah.

2 tablespoons butter

2 slices Vermont cheddar cheese

2 slices Challah (page 185) or other bread

1. Heat a griddle or cast-iron skillet over medium heat. Melt 1 tablespoon of the butter on the surface.

2. Place the cheese between the 2 slices of bread and place it on the buttered surface. Using a spatula, press down on the sandwich.

3. Cook until the sandwich is lightly browned on the bottom, about 4 minutes. (If the bread begins to burn, regulate the heat.)

4. Slip the spatula under the sandwich and drop the remaining tablespoon of butter onto the griddle or cast-iron skillet. When the butter has melted, flip the sandwich and cook the other side, pressing down with the spatula, until it is lightly browned on the other side and the cheese has melted, about 4 additional minutes. Serve immediately.

Variation: To make The Viktor Pinchuk (Ukraine's Second Richest Man), simply layer in 2 thin slices of smoked ham along with the cheese.

THE MILLA JOVOVICH (SUPERMODEL)

GRILLED CHICKEN, VERMONT CHEDDAR, AND ROASTED PEPPERS ON CIABATTA

Serves 4

This is our favorite version of the chicken sandwich. Roasting peppers makes them sweeter and easier to digest. In fact, you may want to roast a whole bunch of them, slice them, and then place them in a dish with some oil. They'll keep in your refrigerator for a while that way, and you'll find they add a little zing to all sorts of dishes.

1 red bell pepper

2 tablespoons butter

4 ciabatta rolls, split

4 Grilled Marinated Chicken
   Breasts (see page 71)

8 slices Vermont cheddar cheese

1. To roast the bell pepper, set a rack about 6 inches from the broiler and preheat the broiler. Place the pepper on an aluminum foil–lined cookie sheet or jelly-roll pan and slide it under the broiler. Let the skin of the pepper char on one side, then turn, using tongs. Repeat until the pepper is evenly charred and has collapsed.

2. Transfer the pepper to a bowl and cover it with plastic wrap. When the pepper is cool enough to handle, stem, peel, and seed it. Cut into strips (if the pepper has not already separated into strips as you're peeling it—they often do) and set aside.

3. To make the sandwich, heat a griddle or cast-iron skillet over medium heat. Melt 1 tablespoon of the butter on the surface.

4. Assemble each sandwich by placing a chicken breast on the bottom, topped with 2 slices of the cheese, topped with a few roasted pepper slices.

5. Place as many sandwiches as will fit on the buttered surface. Using a spatula, press down on the sandwich or sandwiches.

6. Cook until lightly browned on the bottom, about 4 minutes. (If the bread begins to burn, regulate the heat.)

7. Slip the spatula under the sandwich or sandwiches and drop the remaining table-spoon of butter onto the griddle or cast-iron skillet. When the butter has melted, flip the sandwich or sandwiches and cook, pressing down with the spatula, until the other side is lightly browned and the cheese has melted, about 4 more minutes. Repeat with the remaining sandwiches and additional butter, if necessary.

THE LEONID STADNIK (THE WORLD'S TALLEST MAN)

GRILLED KIELBASA ON CIABATTA WITH
HOMEMADE SAUERKRAUT

Serves 4

Leonid Stadnik was a Ukrainian native who was the world's tallest man. We figured at eight feet five inches tall, he'd need a big, meaty sandwich to sate his appetite. Like many sandwiches, this can only be as good as its components, but if you do it right—juicy kielbasa, a crusty roll, homemade sauerkraut—you may be surprised at how delicious and even elegant a kielbasa sandwich can be. Just be sure to have plenty of napkins on hand! You can also split the rolls and toast them on the grill for a minute or two if you like.

4 ciabatta rolls or other crusty rolls

1 pound kielbasa

1 cup Sauerkraut (page 94)

1. Prepare a grill for cooking.
2. Cut the kielbasa in half, if necessary, in order to fit it onto your grill. Slice the kielbasa lengthwise. With a sharp knife, cut crosshatch marks into the skin sides of the sausage.
3. Grill the kielbasa on the grill rack, turning once, until charred with grill marks and heated through, about 2 minutes per side.
4. Split the rolls lengthwise, leaving one long side attached.
5. Cut the kielbasa into 4 pieces and place one piece in each of the 4 rolls. Top each with about ¼ cup sauerkraut and serve immediately.

THE MADAME ALEXANDER (DOLL MANUFACTURER)
ROAST TURKEY, VERMONT CHEDDAR, AND CHIPOTLE
CRANBERRY SAUCE ON RAISIN-FENNEL BREAD

Serves 4

I find most turkey sandwiches served in delis and diners kind of dry and characterless, so when we started selling the Madame Alexander at our kiosk, Little Veselka, in the little park where First Avenue and 1st Street meet, I was determined that ours would be special. We use a semolina bread with raisins and fennel seeds from Amy's Bread, and we spread it with our special spicy and tangy chipotle-cranberry sauce, but perhaps the best thing about this sandwich is the turkey itself: We brine real turkey breasts for twenty-four hours, and then our butcher, Julian Baczynsky, smokes them. The result is a nitrate-free smoked turkey breast that actually tastes of poultry.

One 16-ounce can cranberry sauce

One 7-ounce can chipotle peppers in adobo
    sauce, drained

8 slices raisin-fennel semolina bread

8 thick slices natural smoked turkey breast

8 slices Vermont cheddar cheese

1. Combine the cranberry sauce and the chipotle peppers in a food processor fitted with the metal blade and process until smooth. (If you are highly sensitive to spicy foods, you may want to start with only about half the peppers and add more to taste.) Set aside.

2. Spread 1 to 2 tablespoons of the cranberry-chipotle mixture on 4 of the slices of bread. Top with 2 slices of turkey breast on each. Top the turkey with 2 slices of the cheese on each. Spread additional cranberry-chipotle mixture on the remaining 4 pieces of bread and place them, spread-side down, on the sandwiches. (You will probably have cranberry-chipotle sauce left over. Covered, it will keep in the refrigerator for at least one week.)

3. Serve at room temperature.

8

BREAKFAST ANY TIME

Buttermilk Pancakes

Banana Pancakes

Blueberry Pancakes

Raspberry Pancakes

Buckwheat Pancakes

Buttermilk Waffles

French Toast

Western Omelet

Smoked Salmon Omelet

Broccoli and Vermont Cheddar
  Quiche

Oatmeal

Blueberry Muffins

Raspberry Muffins

Cranberry Walnut Muffins

Whole Wheat Blueberry Muffins

Whole Wheat Apple Muffins

Banana Crunch Muffins

Pumpkin Muffins

Corn Muffins

Blueberry Oat Muffins

Cheese Danish

Cherry Danish

Apple Danish

Scones

AT VESELKA we serve breakfast foods all day, and why not? In fact, it's part of our democratic philosophy: No part of the menu is ever unavailable. And we've been open twenty-four hours a day, seven days a week since spring of 1990. That means if you're in the mood for cabbage soup at sunrise, or craving blintzes in the middle of the night, you're in luck. Our breakfast specialties include waffles, pancakes, and challah French toast, all perfect with a cup of coffee and a stack of newspapers.

There is one popular item on the Veselka breakfast menu that is not represented here: our flaky, delicious croissants. We serve about 45 croissants every morning at Veselka, and they're all made in-house, but as hard as we tried, there was simply no adapting tricky croissant dough (which needs to be made with cold butter) for the home kitchen. You'll just have to come to Veselka for your croissant fix.

Like a lot of people, I think, the first things I ever cooked at home were breakfast foods—scrambled eggs, pancakes, bacon. I've always felt that if a restaurant serves a good breakfast, it's halfway to being successful. People really like to go out for breakfast. When my father-in-law passed away in the 1970s and I took over the restaurant, I redid the menu, and I came up with some pretty simple breakfast dishes based on what I like to eat. At the time there was a guy working here named Jack Linn—he's now chief of operations for the New York City Department of Parks & Recreation and still lives up the street. Jack said to me, "Tom, look, You've got to do two things: You've got to have good coffee, and you've got to have good bacon." It turns out he was right on target. In general I don't try to save money on ingredients, but that's doubly true for breakfast. We buy good eggs, good bacon,

Veselka customers seated below the mural by Arnie Charnick. *(Ben Fink)*

good ham, and we always use real butter and not margarine. People don't necessarily notice the individual ingredients, but they go away saying what a great breakfast they had.

Breakfast turned Veselka around financially, too. At the time I took over, I'd never run a business before. I was a kid in my twenties, and I really didn't know what I was doing. At one point we sold all kinds of things besides food to try and make ends meet: stationery and pens and lottery tickets and paper clips and those pink rubber "spaldeen" balls people once used for stickball. It also wasn't a great time economically for New York City in general and for this neighborhood in particular. People didn't have a lot of extra money to spend.

Once I'd overhauled the menu and brought in good ingredients, though, breakfast became a big part of our business. Up until then, we'd been known basically as a place for borscht, pierogi, and blintzes and that was about it, and we weren't well-known beyond the Ukrainian community. But word spread that we were serving something you couldn't get at the diner on your corner, or, as Liz Logan put it in a 1990 article for *House & Garden*, "A Veselka breakfast is to a standard coffee shop breakfast as the Chrysler Building is to the Pan Am Building." When we started to see customers from other neighborhoods actually traveling to Veselka for breakfast, I knew things were looking up. Today, Saturday is our busiest day of the week, and at breakfast time it's really hopping. We don't take any reservations, and there's always a long line in the mornings on the weekend. During the week it's busy, too—on a typical weekday we serve 800 to 1,000 people—but on weekends people tend to sit longer, and they also eat breakfast all day on Saturdays and Sundays (we don't use the word brunch, but I suppose that's what it is). I love those moments, and not just because seats are full. There's a special buzz to a weekend breakfast at Veselka, when coffee mugs are being refilled and plates of fluffy pancakes are coming out of the kitchen at a rapid rate. That's when I most feel it's the low-key, friendly gathering place I dreamed of creating.

The Birth and Growth of Veselka

Veselka is one-of-a-kind. We've never opened various outlets (unless you count Little Veselka, the kiosk in First Park that sells soups and sandwiches and breakfast fare from the restaurant, but that's not exactly a restaurant). In fact, Veselka has been located on the same corner since it opened in 1954.

When Wolodymyr Darmochwal and his wife, Olha, opened Veselka that year, it wasn't actually a restaurant. It was the kind of candy shop/newsstand that you could find on many corners in New York City at the time. Those stores sold everything from newspapers to pens and pencils to loose cigarettes. Veselka had a lunch counter and a few employees, but it was nothing close to an actual restaurant. It wasn't run efficiently, either: At the original Veselka, someone took your order, made the food, then cleared your dishes, washed them, and put them away. It was basically the unofficial canteen for Plast, the Ukrainian scouting organization upstairs (Wolodymyr was a lifelong and proud member of Plast, and today there is a dining hall named for him at a Plast camp in Ukraine), and it was only a fraction of the size that it is now.

Shortly after Veselka opened, a place next door that sold very inexpensive steaks went out of business, and Veselka absorbed that area and inherited a

That's me on the right and Michael Hrynenko on the left behind the Veselka cash register in 1974. On the shelf behind us are some of the many items we used to sell, including Vaseline, shaving cream, and aspirin. Michael went on to open the Ukrainian restaurant Kiev, which has since closed, a couple of blocks away. *(Author's Collection)*

kitchen in the process. When I first came to Veselka in 1967, it consisted solely of what is now the front room: a counter with stools and four or five tables. But Wolodymyr was already in the process of taking over the shop next door— a button shop owned by a woman who apparently was very wealthy and lived on Fifth Avenue, but ran the store to keep busy. I helped clean out the space, and I can still picture the way every inch in there was covered with buttons, from floor to ceiling.

That expansion gave Veselka a little more space and its first real dining area, though the dining room remained "by invitation only," meaning if you were Ukrainian or Wolodymyr liked you, he'd let you in. He started letting up on that as time went on, and then when he passed away in 1975, I opened up the dining room to anyone who wanted to sit there. Physically, though, going back there still felt a little like visiting a speakeasy—you had to shimmy through a narrow passageway, and there were heavy blue drapes in the window, so no one outside would have guessed it was a restaurant. In the early 1980s, we got our first dishwasher, which was very exciting to all the workers whose hands had grown chapped here over the years. Later on, we installed a beer tap and I reconfigured the counter area a little. Looking back, I can see that I was always struggling to help the physical plant keep up with the business, which was growing by leaps and bounds, but when you're in the thick of it, sometimes it's hard to get a clear picture.

Then, in 1996, when I'd owned the restaurant for twenty years, I had an opportunity to acquire the space next door as well, and I took it. We shut down for three and a half months. The goal was to make the place feel a little more open and airy and, frankly, cleaner. The dining room expanded to just over 2,000 square feet to hold seats for ninety-five people. I'm happy to say that those seats are almost always full, as is the outdoor seating area, which was added at the same time. It may sound odd, since I'd been the boss for two decades at that point, but that was when I truly began to consider Veselka my own restaurant.

Still, running a business is always a balancing act, and that's doubly true for a place like Veselka. For some reason— whether it's the neighborhood, the kind of restaurant Veselka is, or something else—we have a lot of customers who are very averse to change. You want to continue to broaden your audience, but you also don't want to turn off the regulars. When we were closed down in 1996, some of our more eccentric

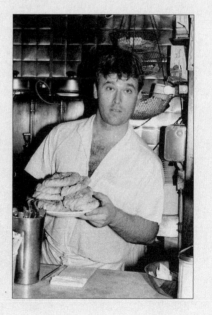

Bobby worked as a dishwasher at Veselka for several years in the 1980s. *(Author's Collection)*

regular customers didn't believe we'd ever reopen—I had to be like a therapist to them and reassure them almost daily.

Then, when the work was done and we reopened, one long-time customer came to me and said, "Veselka is corporate now. You've made it all flashy. I'm not going to come anymore." That's a little hard to hear when you've spent nearly half a million dollars on renovations, but I needn't have worried: By the following week, that customer was back in his usual spot at the counter at his usual time.

Now, as I'm putting the finishing touches on this book, we're expanding Veselka one more time. The store that used to be next door is moving over one more storefront, and we'll gain another 400 square feet or so. We're not closing this time, but it's agonizing in its own way. I always imagine that renovating—whether it's your business or your home that's under the knife— is sort of like having a baby, in that while you're doing it it feels terrible, but you're so happy with the results that you forget all the pain that went into it.

The big plate-glass window at the front of Veselka looks out onto Second Avenue. *(Ben Fink)*

BUTTERMILK PANCAKES

Makes 12 to 14 large pancakes; about 6 servings

Pancakes are one of the most popular dishes at Veselka and definitely our breakfast bestseller. The buttermilk makes these extra fluffy, and the combination of durum flour (the kind of flour used to make dried pasta) and superlight cake flour gives them the perfect texture. Like muffin and quick-bread batters and scone dough, pancake batter does not like to be handled too much—mix the wet and dry ingredients just until they are combined. Any lumps remaining in the batter will smooth out on their own as the pancakes cook. I've given a range for the buttermilk because it can vary depending on the weather, how old your flour is, and so forth. Begin by using the smaller amount and add more if you need it. These are great the classic way—with butter and maple syrup—and also delicious when topped with fruit, such as sliced strawberries and bananas.

2 cups durum (semolina) flour

2 cups cake flour

5 tablespoons sugar

1½ teaspoons baking powder

1 tablespoon plus 1 teaspoon baking soda

¼ cup cornmeal

1 teaspoon salt

5 large eggs

2¾ to 3 cups buttermilk

½ cup vegetable oil

1 tablespoon vanilla extract

Unsalted butter or oil, for greasing the
  griddle

1. In a large bowl, combine both the flours, sugar, baking powder, baking soda, cornmeal, and salt. Whisk to combine.

2. In a medium bowl, combine the eggs, 2¾ cups buttermilk, oil, and vanilla and beat to combine.

3. Pour the wet ingredients into the dry ingredients. Mix briefly with a wooden spoon. The batter should have a loose, pourable consistency so that it will spread when you put it on the griddle. Add more buttermilk, if needed.

4. Place a griddle or cast-iron skillet over medium heat and heat until a few drops of water sprinkled on the surface dance and sizzle. Grease the surface of the griddle with a small amount of butter or oil. (Using a paper towel is the easiest way to do

this.) Using a soup ladle or measuring cup, drop about ½ cup of the batter onto the griddle. (We use a 4-ounce ice cream scoop, which works perfectly.)

5. Let the pancake cook until small bubbles begin to appear on the surface and the underside is nicely browned, about 2 minutes, adjusting the heat if necessary. Flip the pancake with a spatula and cook the other side until it is cooked through and nicely browned.

6. Remove the finished pancake and repeat with remaining batter. You may want to keep the pancakes warm in a 200°F oven until you are ready to serve them.

Variations: For Banana Pancakes, stir about 2 large bananas, sliced, into the batter before making the pancakes, at the end of step 3. For Blueberry Pancakes or Raspberry Pancakes, toss 1 cup of berries with the dry ingredients in step 1.

BUCKWHEAT PANCAKES

Makes 12 to 14 large pancakes; about 6 servings

Flour made from buckwheat, which is actually a grass, not a grain, adds a hearty flavor to all kinds of foods, including pancakes. Just as with plain buttermilk pancakes, you don't want to overmix these.

2 cups buckwheat flour

2 cups cake flour

5 tablespoons sugar

2½ tablespoons baking powder

¼ cup yellow cornmeal

2 teaspoons salt

2 to 2¼ cups whole milk

3 large eggs

½ cup vegetable oil

1 tablespoon vanilla extract

Unsalted butter or oil, for greasing the
   griddle

1. In a large bowl, combine both the flours, sugar, baking powder, cornmeal, and salt. Whisk to combine.

2. In a medium bowl, combine 2 cups milk, eggs, oil, and vanilla and beat to combine.

3. Pour the wet ingredients into the dry ingredients. Mix briefly with a wooden spoon. The batter should have a loose, pourable consistency so that it will spread when you put it on the griddle. Add more milk, if needed.

4. Place a griddle or cast-iron skillet over medium heat and heat until a few drops of water sprinkled on the surface dance and sizzle. Grease the surface of the griddle with a small amount of butter or oil. (Using a paper towel is the easiest way to do this.) Using a soup ladle or measuring cup, drop about ½ cup of the batter onto the griddle. (We use a 4-ounce ice cream scoop, which works perfectly.)

5. Let the pancake cook until small bubbles begin to appear on the surface and the underside is nicely browned, about 2 minutes; adjusting the heat, if necessary. Flip the pancake with a spatula and cook the other side until it is cooked through and nicely browned.

6. Remove the finished pancake and repeat with remaining batter. You may want to keep the pancakes warm in a 200°F oven until you are ready to serve them.

BUTTERMILK WAFFLES

Makes about 6 waffles; about 2 servings

Tangy buttermilk makes these waffles fluffy and delicious. At the restaurant we buy special waffle flour from Carbon's (see Resources on page 249), which has some leavening and sugar already incorporated. The mixture is pretty easy to throw together at home, though, so we've figured out a recipe for it here. If you like, you could do what we do and keep the dry ingredients on hand in bulk, then just add the wet ingredients when you're ready to make waffles. These are great with macerated berries on top.

1½ cups all-purpose flour

1 tablespoon sugar

1 tablespoon baking powder

1 cup buttermilk

2 large eggs

4 tablespoons unsalted butter, melted

1 teaspoon vanilla extract

1. In a large bowl, combine the flour, sugar, and baking powder and mix with a whisk or fork to incorporate.
2. In a liquid measuring cup with a spout, beat the buttermilk, eggs, butter, and vanilla.
3. Pour the wet ingredients into the dry ingredients and mix just until combined. Do not overmix.
4. Cook the waffles in a hot waffle iron until golden brown. Serve immediately.

FRENCH TOAST

Serves 4

French toast is a humble dish invented as a way to use up leftover stale bread, but we elevate it with some half-and-half, cinnamon, and vanilla. Quicker than pancakes, a few slices of French toast make any weekday breakfast special—especially if you've got our homemade Challah on hand. Serve with maple syrup and perhaps some sliced fruit.

6 large eggs, lightly beaten

2 cups half-and-half

1 teaspoon cinnamon

2 teaspoons vanilla extract

12 slices Challah (page 185)

Unsalted butter or oil, for greasing the griddle

1. Combine the eggs, half-and-half, cinnamon, and vanilla in a wide, shallow bowl. Beat until frothy.
2. Place the challah in the egg mixture and turn a couple times until the bread has softened.
3. Place a griddle or cast-iron skillet over medium heat and heat until a few drops of water sprinkled on the surface dance and sizzle. Grease the surface of the griddle with a small amount of butter or oil. (Using a paper towel is the easiest way to do this.)
4. Cook as many slices of bread as you can fit in the pan in one layer. Cook until browned on one side, about 3 minutes, then turn and cook until browned on the other side. Serve hot.

WESTERN OMELET

Serves 2

Don't be intimidated by omelets—they're really just scrambled eggs. This recipe makes one large omelet, which will feed two people. This is more of a diner-style omelet than the French classic type, meaning it doesn't have a filling (the ham and peppers and onion are mixed into the eggs) and it's cooked until fairly dry, while a French omelet is left very moist in the center.

6 large eggs	¼ cup diced red bell pepper
2 tablespoons whole milk	¼ cup diced ham
Salt	2 tablespoons chopped onion
Freshly ground black pepper	1 tablespoon unsalted butter

1. In a medium bowl, whisk the eggs and milk until fluffy. Season to taste with salt and pepper. Stir in the bell pepper, ham, and onions.
2. Heat a nonstick frying pan or omelet pan over medium heat. Add butter to pan, and when the butter has melted, tilt the pan to coat the entire surface with butter, then pour in the egg mixture.
3. Use a fork to stir the egg mixture and gently tug in the cooked bits and mix them with the uncooked egg until the bottom begins to set. Then let the eggs cook, untouched, until the bottom is browned.
4. Run a spatula under the bottom of the omelet, slide the omelet out onto a large plate, then turn it back into the pan, upside down, and cook until the other side browns, about 2 minutes.
5. Again run a spatula under the bottom and fold the omelet in half. Transfer to a plate and serve immediately. (With a little practice, you should be able to fold the omelet and turn it out of the pan and onto the plate at the same time.)

Variation: To make a Smoked Salmon Omelet, replace the bell peppers, ham, and onion with ½ cup of diced smoked salmon.

BROCCOLI AND VERMONT CHEDDAR QUICHE

Serves 6

When you're having guests for brunch, or even lunch, quiche is a great option. You can make it in advance, it cooks all at once (as opposed to pancakes or omelets), and it feels a little more festive than plain scrambled eggs. We use Cabot brand cheddar cheese for this dish and any others that include cheddar.

CRUST

1½ cups all-purpose flour

¾ teaspoon salt

1 stick (8 tablespoons) *very cold* unsalted
   butter, cut into cubes

¼ to ½ cup ice water

FILLING

2 cups roughly chopped broccoli

1 cup grated Vermont cheddar cheese

1 large tomato, seeded and chopped

6 large eggs

¾ cup heavy cream

½ teaspoon freshly ground black pepper

½ teaspoon dried oregano

¼ teaspoon salt

1. To make the crust, place the flour and salt in a medium bowl and stir to combine. Cut in the butter, using a pastry blender or two knives, until the mixture resembles coarse meal. Do not overwork—you want little pebbles of butter to remain.

2. Sprinkle ¼ cup of the ice water over the flour and butter mixture and stir with a fork just until the dough forms a ball. Again, do not overwork the dough. Add a little more ice water in small amounts if needed, until the dough forms a ball.

3. Pat the dough into a rough disk, wrap in plastic, and chill in the refrigerator for 30 minutes. While the dough is chilling, preheat the oven to 425°F.

4. On a well-floured work surface, roll the dough out into a circle slightly larger than a 9-inch pie plate. Transfer the dough to a 9-inch pie plate and trim the overhang. Crimp the edges.

5. Line the shell with aluminum foil and fill with pie weights, then bake in the preheated oven 15 minutes. Remove foil and weights and bake until lightly browned,

about 5 additional minutes. Remove from the oven and set aside to cool. Lower the oven temperature to 350°F.

6. While the crust is cooling, blanch the broccoli just until tender. Run cold water over the broccoli, drain, and then cut it into small dice.

7. Set the pie crust, still in the pan, on a cookie sheet or jelly-roll pan. Spread the broccoli, grated cheese, and chopped tomato evenly over the bottom of the cooled pie crust.

8. In a small bowl, whisk together the eggs, cream, black pepper, oregano, and salt. Pour the egg mixture over the cheese and vegetables.

9. Bake the quiche until the custard is set and browned on top, about 45 minutes. If the edges of the crust begin to look too dark but the filling is not yet set, cover the edges with aluminum foil. Serve the quiche warm or at room temperature.

OATMEAL

Serves 2

At Veselka, we serve some very basic dishes, such as fried eggs, oatmeal, and tuna fish sand-wiches. Yet I hear from customers over and over that these dishes, which are easy enough to make at home, "just taste better" at Veselka.

*Case in point: One Veselka customer goes to the same gym that I do, and he approached me in the locker room one day and told me that he'd tried to make oatmeal at home, but he just couldn't match Veselka's oatmeal. What was in it that was so special? (He's not the only one who appreciates our oatmeal—*The New York Times *has named it the best oatmeal in New York City.)*

I explained that we use half milk and half water for the liquid, and perhaps that was giving the oatmeal its unique flavor. He nodded thoughtfully, and a couple days later I ran into him again. He'd tried the half milk and half water method, but still, the oatmeal at Veselka just tasted better than his own. Had he let it sit before serving it? He shook his head and went on his way. A few days later, same story. This went on for several weeks, with my going over the Veselka oatmeal method with him every time we encountered each other, and finally, after eight or ten tries, he came to me with a big smile and said he'd gotten it just right—but he still orders oatmeal at Veselka. Go figure.

1 cup whole milk

1 cup rolled oats

Pinch salt

1. In a small pot, combine the milk with 1 cup water and bring to a boil.
2. Sprinkle in the oatmeal very gradually. Stir to mix. Add the salt and stir again.
3. When the liquid returns to a boil, turn down to a simmer and cook, stirring frequently, until the oats are tender and all the liquid has been absorbed, about 5 minutes.
4. When the oats are cooked, cover the pot and set aside off the heat for 5 minutes.
5. Serve with raisins, walnuts, honey, maple syrup, sliced fruit, and anything else you like.

BLUEBERRY MUFFINS

Makes 12 large muffins

These are big, rich muffins—probably big enough that one could be considered breakfast for two people, or one very hungry person. Warm from the oven, perhaps split and buttered or smeared with a little jam, they are a great treat. We also make Blueberry Oat Muffins (page 233) that have a little less fat and may be a better choice for everyday eating. This recipe, like all the muffin recipes in this book, is incredibly versatile. It makes enough batter for 12 jumbo-size muffins, 24 regular muffins, or two 9-x-4-inch quick-bread loaves.

2 sticks (16 tablespoons) unsalted butter

2½ cups sugar

2 teaspoons vanilla extract

4 large eggs

4 cups all-purpose flour

3¾ teaspoons baking powder

1 teaspoon salt

1 cup buttermilk

1½ cups blueberries, rinsed and dried on
    paper towels, or 1½ cups frozen
    blueberries

1. Preheat the oven to 350°F. Place paper muffin cups in 12 indentations in extra-large muffin pans and set aside. (Alternatively, spray the indentations with non-stick cooking spray and dust with flour.)

2. In the large bowl of a stand mixer (or in a large bowl using a handheld mixer), cream together the butter and sugar until light and fluffy, about 3 minutes. Beat in the vanilla and eggs.

3. In a medium bowl, whisk together the flour, baking powder, and salt.

4. Add about one-third of the flour mixture to the butter and egg mixture and beat smooth, then add about one-third of the buttermilk and beat smooth. Continue to alternate with two more additions of each, beating smooth between additions until the flour mixture and buttermilk have been incorporated.

5. Using a rubber spatula, gently fold in the blueberries.

6. Spoon the batter into the prepared muffin tins, filling them each by about two-thirds full, and bake in the preheated oven until muffin tops are dry and spring

back when pressed lightly with a fingertip and a tester inserted in the centers comes out dry, about 35 minutes.

7. Cool the muffins in the pans on racks for 5 minutes, then unmold and leave on racks to cool completely. Store in airtight tins.

Variations: *For Raspberry Muffins, replace the blueberries with an equal amount of raspberries. For Cranberry Walnut Muffins, replace the blueberries with 1½ cups cranberries and fold in ½ cup chopped walnuts in step 5 as well. Sprinkle the tops of the muffins with a small amount of additional sugar before baking. For Whole Wheat Blueberry Muffins, replace 2 cups of all-purpose flour with whole wheat flour. For Whole Wheat Apple Muffins, replace 2 cups of all-purpose flour with whole wheat flour, and replace the blueberries with 1 large green apple, diced with peel, and ¾ cup golden raisins. Reserve a handful of diced apple and sprinkle it on the tops of the muffins.*

BANANA CRUNCH MUFFINS

Makes 12 large muffins

These are yet another variation on the Blueberry Muffins above, with bananas and walnuts in place of the berries and a crunchy streusel topping.

CRUMB TOPPING

½ cup brown sugar, firmly packed

1¼ cups all-purpose flour

2 tablespoons rolled oats

¼ teaspoon ground cinnamon

¾ teaspoon baking powder

8 tablespoons (1 stick) unsalted butter

BATTER

2 sticks (16 tablespoons) unsalted butter

2½ cups sugar

2 teaspoons vanilla extract

4 large eggs

4 cups all-purpose flour

3¾ teaspoons baking powder

1 teaspoon salt

1 cup buttermilk

2 large bananas, sliced

¾ cup chopped walnuts

1. To make the crumb topping, place all ingredients in a small bowl. Cut in the butter, using your fingertips or a pastry blender, until the mixture resembles small pebbles. Chill while preparing the muffin batter.

2. Preheat the oven to 350°F. Place paper muffin cups in 12 indentations in extra-large muffin pans and set aside. (Alternatively, spray the indentations with non-stick cooking spray and dust with flour.)

3. In the large bowl of a stand mixer (or in a large bowl using a handheld mixer), cream together the butter and sugar until light and fluffy, about 3 minutes. Beat in the vanilla and eggs.

3. In a medium bowl, whisk together the flour, baking powder, and salt.

4. Add about one-third of the flour mixture to the butter and egg mixture and beat smooth, then add about one-third of the buttermilk and beat smooth. Continue to alternate with two more additions of each, beating smooth between additions, until the flour mixture and buttermilk have been incorporated.

5. Using a rubber spatula, gently fold in the banana slices and walnuts.

6. Spoon the batter into the prepared muffin tins, filling them each by about two-thirds full. Sprinkle the crumb topping over the muffins and bake in the pre-heated oven until muffin tops are dry and spring back when pressed lightly with a fingertip and a tester inserted in the centers comes out dry, about 35 minutes.

7. Cool the muffins in the pans on racks for 5 minutes, then unmold and leave on the racks to cool completely. Store in airtight tins.

PUMPKIN MUFFINS

Makes 12 large muffins

We don't use a lot of canned products at Veselka, but—like many bakers—pastry chef Lisa Straub relies on canned pumpkin for making muffins. Canned pumpkin is so much more consistent than fresh, steamed pumpkin, and not many supermarkets carry true "pie pumpkins" anymore. Make sure you buy plain pumpkin purée and not canned pumpkin pie filling, which has sugar and spices added to it. One 15-ounce can should give you just about the 1½ cups you need for this recipe.

1¾ cups plus 1 tablespoon rolled oats

1½ cups all-purpose flour

1½ teaspoons baking powder

¾ teaspoon baking soda

1¼ cups light brown sugar, firmly packed

1½ teaspoons ground cinnamon

¾ teaspoon salt

¾ cups chopped pecans

1 cup chocolate chips

One 15-ounce can pumpkin purée (about 1½ cups)

¾ cups vegetable oil

½ cup whole milk

2 large eggs

1 tablespoon vanilla extract

1. Preheat oven to 350°F. Place paper muffin cups in 12 indentations in extra-large muffin pans and set aside. (Alternatively, spray the indentations with nonstick cooking spray and dust with flour.)

2. In a large bowl, combine the 1¾ cups oats, flour, baking powder, baking soda, brown sugar, cinnamon, and salt. Whisk briefly to combine.

3. Add the pecans and chocolate chips to the bowl and toss to combine with the other dry ingredients.

4. In a medium bowl, combine the pumpkin purée, oil, milk, eggs, and vanilla. Beat with a fork until incorporated.

5. Pour the wet ingredients into the dry ingredients and mix with a wooden spoon just until all the dry ingredients have been moistened. Do not overbeat.

6. Spoon the batter into the prepared muffin tins, filling them each by about two-thirds full. Sprinkle the remaining 1 tablespoon rolled oats on the tops of the

muffins and bake in the preheated oven until muffin tops are dry and spring back when pressed lightly with a fingertip and a tester inserted in the centers comes out dry, about 35 minutes.

7. Cool the muffins in the pans on racks for 5 minutes, then unmold and leave on the racks to cool completely. Store in airtight tins.

CORN MUFFINS

Makes 12 large muffins

Corn muffins are made slightly differently from other muffins. They're really individual cornbreads baked in muffin tins. That means they have more brown crispy edges, which I think is the best part of a corn muffin.

4¼ cups cake flour

2 cups sugar

2 cups yellow cornmeal

1 tablespoon plus 1 teaspoon baking
   powder

4 large eggs

2 sticks (16 tablespoons) unsalted butter,
   melted

1 tablespoon vanilla extract

1½ cups buttermilk

1. Preheat the oven to 350°F. Place paper muffin cups in 12 indentations in extra-large muffin pans and set aside. (Alternatively, spray the indentations with non-stick cooking spray and dust with flour.)
2. In a large bowl, combine the flour, sugar, cornmeal, and baking powder.
3. In a medium bowl or large measuring cup, beat together the eggs, melted butter, vanilla, and buttermilk.
4. Make a well in the center of the dry ingredients and pour in the wet ingredients. Stir with a wooden spoon just until combined. Do not overmix.
5. Spoon the batter into the prepared muffin tins, filling them each by about two-thirds full, and bake in the preheated oven until muffin tops are dry and spring back when pressed lightly with a fingertip and a tester inserted in the centers comes out dry, about 35 minutes
6. Cool the muffins in the pans on racks for 5 minutes, then unmold and leave on the racks to cool completely. Store in airtight tins.

BLUEBERRY OAT MUFFINS

Makes 12 large muffins

These are a heartier muffin than our original Blueberry Muffins (page 226) due to the inclusion of oat bran and rolled oats. (Be sure to use rolled oats, sometimes labeled oat flakes, not instant oatmeal or steel-cut oats.) They're still delicious, but have a completely different texture than the others.

2 cups all-purpose flour

1 cup oat bran

1 cup rolled oats

¾ cup sugar

1 tablespoon baking powder

1 teaspoon salt

4 egg whites

8 tablespoons (1 stick) unsalted butter, melted

½ cup orange juice

1 cup buttermilk (maybe a touch more)

1 tablespoons vanilla extract

1½ cups blueberries, rinsed and dried on paper towels, or 1½ cups frozen blueberries

1. Preheat the oven to 350°F. Place paper muffin cups in 12 indentations in extra-large muffin pans and set aside. (Alternatively, spray the indentations with non-stick cooking spray and dust with flour.)

2. In a large bowl, combine the flour, oat bran, ½ cup of the rolled oats, sugar, baking powder, and salt.

3. In a medium bowl or large measuring cup, beat together the egg whites, melted butter, orange juice, buttermilk, and vanilla.

4. Make a well in the center of the dry ingredients and pour in the wet ingredients. Stir with a wooden spoon just until combined. Do not overmix.

5. Using a rubber spatula, gently fold in the blueberries.

6. Spoon the batter into the prepared muffin tins, filling them each by about two-thirds full. Sprinkle the remaining ½ cup rolled oats on top of the muffins and bake in the preheated oven until muffin tops are dry and spring back when pressed lightly with a fingertip and a tester inserted in the centers comes out dry.

7. Cool the muffins in the pans on racks for 5 minutes, then unmold and leave on racks to cool completely. Store in airtight tins.

CHEESE DANISH

Makes 18 pastries

If you've only eaten bakery Danish before, the homemade pastries will be a revelation. The butter is crucial to this buttery dough. Make sure you use a European-style butter (Plugrá is widely available in supermarkets), which should be soft, but not supersoft. Usually 30 minutes at room temperature will get the butter to the right consistency. The goal is for it to be pliable as you incorporate it into the dough, but not so mushy that it smears all over the place. European-style butters have a lower moisture content and more butterfat than regular supermarket butter, so they result in much flakier Danish. Because the dough is so buttery, and because you don't want the butter to be incorporated into the dough but to remain in little chunks, it is crucial that you not allow the dough to become overheated. Leave yourself a lot of time when making Danish, and refrigerate it any time the dough becomes too soft. Refrigerating or freezing it at each step may be necessary, especially in a warm kitchen. Danish dough cannot be rushed, and this recipe is not for the novice baker.

You can also make the dough in advance and freeze it as a whole log or after it has been cut into pinwheels. Just thaw it in the refrigerator overnight and bake it straight out of the refrigerator in the morning. That way you can have fresh, hot pastry in the morning without getting up in the middle of the night to make it.

1 tablespoon unsalted butter, room
 temperature

¼ cup plus 1 tablespoon sugar

2 tablespoons cornstarch

1 large egg

Zest of 1 lemon

½ teaspoon vanilla extract

12 ounces cream cheese, room temperature,
 cut into 8 pieces

FINISHING

Egg wash: 1 large egg, lightly beaten

2½ teaspoons ground cinnamon

¾ cup sugar

1 cup raisins

Apricot glaze: 1 cup apricot jam, warmed
 with a few teaspoons of water to soften

DOUGH

1½ cups plus 2 tablespoons whole milk

6 large eggs, beaten

2 tablespoons sour cream

1 tablespoon plus 1 teaspoon instant yeast

1 cup sugar

1½ teaspoons ground cardamom

2 teaspoons lemon extract

2 teaspoons orange extract

1 tablespoon vanilla extract

9 cups bread flour

2 teaspoons salt

¼ cup vegetable oil

1¼ pounds (5 sticks) European-style
 unsalted butter such as Plugrá, softened
 slightly

1. To make the filling, in the bowl of an electric mixer fitted with the paddle attachment, mix the butter, sugar, and cornstarch until sandy. Add the egg,
lemon zest, and vanilla. Add the cream cheese one piece at a time, waiting
until each piece is incorporated before you add another. Mix on high speed
until smooth, 1 to 2 minutes. Transfer to a small bowl, cover with plastic

wrap, and refrigerate until ready to use. (The filling can be prepared 1 to 2 days in advance.)

2. To make the dough, in the large bowl of an electric mixer fitted with the dough hook, combine the milk, eggs, sour cream, yeast, sugar, cardamom, and extracts.

3. Place the bowl on the mixer and at low speed add about 7½ cups of the flour, the salt, and the vegetable oil. Mix until the dough comes together, about 3 minutes. Add a little more flour, 1 tablespoon at a time, if the dough seems too liquid and sticky. (It should be slightly tacky to the touch, but should form a mass.)

4. On a well-floured surface using a well-floured rolling pin, roll out the dough to a rectangle ¼- to ½-inch thick and 14 inches × 22 inches. Using a floured rolling pin, pound (do not roll) the butter into a rectangle about ½ inch thick and 12 inches × 10 inches (depending on the temperature of your kitchen, you may want to flour the butter). Cut the rectangle of butter in half the short way.

5. Place one of the two rectangles of pounded butter slightly off-center down the middle of the dough. (It's helpful to visualize the dough as cut in thirds—you want to center the butter in the middle section. See illustration on page 237.) Fold half of the dough over the butter to cover it completely, but the dough will not cover the other half of the dough completely.

6. Place the second half of the flattened butter on top of the fold perpendicular to the first piece of butter. Fold the remaining half of the dough over the butter to cover completely. Press the dough along its perimeter to seal thoroughly. Turn the dough 90 degrees.

7. Reflour your work surface and rolling pin. Roll out the dough again to ¼- to ½-inch thick and 14 inches × 22 inches and fold in thirds. Turn the dough and repeat the rolling and folding process, folding in thirds each time, two more times, flouring as needed. If at any time during this process the dough begins to get so soft that it's hard to work with, simply wrap it in plastic wrap and refrigerate it for 15 to 30 minutes to firm it up again.

8. Preheat the oven to 325°F. Line four jelly-roll pans with parchment paper and set aside.

9. On a floured surface, roll out the dough to a rectangle ¼- to ½-inch thick and 24 inches × 14 inches, brush with egg wash (reserve remaining egg wash), and sprinkle with the cinnamon, sugar, and raisins. Roll jelly-roll style into a log. Cut into 1-inch slices. (The dough will shrink slightly as it is cut, so after you cut the slices they will be closer to ½ inch, but if the log is squishing as you attempt to cut it, refrigerate or freeze it to firm it up before continuing.) Place the slices on their sides on the prepared pans. Cover loosely with plastic wrap and let the Danish sit at room temperature until doubled in size, 20 to 30 minutes. (This may vary a little more widely depending on the temperature of the room.)

10. Make a 1-inch indentation in the center of each piece and fill with about 1 tablespoon of the cheese filling. Brush with the remaining egg wash.

11. Bake the Danish until golden brown, 15 to 20 minutes. Brush with apricot glaze. Cool on baking pans, then store in a tightly sealed container.

Variations: For Cherry Danish, use about one-fourth of the filling from the Cherry Crumb Pies (page 147) in place of the cheese filling. For Apple Danish, peel and slice 2 or 3 large apples and toss them with cinnamon and sugar to taste and use that mixture in place of the cheese filling.

Danish

24" dough

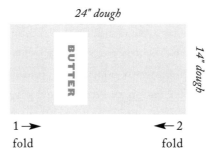

14" dough

1 → fold   ← 2 fold

SCONES

Makes 8 large scones

Scones are the new muffins, or something like that. Americans have fallen in love with the crumbly consistency of scones in the last few years. There are three tricks to making great scones: Start with ice-cold butter, do not overwork the dough, and do not overbake. That ¼ cup of baking powder isn't a typo—scones require a large amount of baking powder to achieve the proper consistency. Just make sure there are no clumps in the powder and that it combines thoroughly with the flour and sugar in step 2. If you'd like to gild the lily, add 1 cup of dried cherries, chopped semisweet chocolate, and/or chopped nuts to these.

3½ cups cake flour

¼ cup baking powder

½ cup sugar, plus more for sprinkling on top
 of the scones

12 tablespoons (1½ sticks) cold unsalted
 butter, cubed

1½ cups heavy cream

1. Preheat the oven to 325°F. Line a cookie sheet with parchment paper and set aside.
2. Place the flour, baking powder, and ½ cup sugar in the bowl of a stand mixer fitted with the paddle attachment and whisk briefly by hand to combine.
3. Add the butter to the bowl and place the bowl on the mixer. Mix until the mixture resembles dry sand, and the chunks of butter are no smaller than peas. (Alternatively, do this by hand using a pastry blender or two knives.)
4. With the machine running, slowly pour in the cream. Be sure to let some of the cream go all the way to the bottom of the bowl so it will incorporate evenly. (Alternatively, do this by hand: Fold in the cream with a spatula, then mix briefly with a fork.) Mix just until the ingredients are combined. Do not overmix.
5. Use a tablespoon to drop the dough in 8 portions onto the prepared cookie sheets. Sprinkle the tops of the scones generously with sugar.
6. Bake the scones until they are just beginning to color but still look slightly underdone, about 20 minutes. Slide the parchment paper with the scones to racks to cool.

MENUS

The recipes that are included book can be found on the page numbers in parentheses following the recipe title.

SUMMER COOKOUT

The Leonid Stadnik *(page 207)*

Turkey Burgers *(page 201)*

Coleslaw *(page 93)*

Chef's Salad *(page 88)*

Blueberry Tarts *(page 149)*

lemonade

UKRAINIAN INDEPENDENCE DAY

(AUGUST 24)

Cold Borscht *(page 15)*

Potato Pierogi *(page 40)*

Grilled Ukrainian Kielbasa *(page 66)*

Sauerkraut *(page 94)*

Ukrainian Poppy Seed Cake *(page 138)*

BUFFET BRUNCH

Meat-Stuffed Cabbage *(page 51)*

Broccoli and Vermont Cheddar Quiche
   (page 223)

French Toast *(page 221)*

Blueberry Muffins *(page 226)*

Rugelach *(page 125)*

PICNIC LUNCH

Cold Borscht *(page 15)*

The Andy Warhola, cut into small squares
   (page 194)

Coleslaw *(page 93)*

Vegetable Pâté *(page 92)*

Corn Muffins *(page 232)*

Raspberry-Apricot Bars *(page 121)*

BOX LUNCH

The Leon Trotsky *(page 195)*

carrot and celery sticks

Oatmeal Raisin Cookies *(page 118)*

HOME WITH A COLD LUNCH

Chicken Noodle Soup *(page 18)*

Whole Wheat Bread *(page 187)*

Brownies *(page 123)*

hot tea with lemon and honey

SUNDAY SUPPER

Split Pea Soup *(page 24)*

The Milla Jovovich *(page 205)*

braised carrots

Rice Pudding *(page 129)*

WEEKNIGHT DINNER

Grilled Marinated Chicken Breasts
   (page 71)

East Village Spinach Salad *(page 86)*

M&M Cookies *(page 119)*

SUPERBOWL PARTY

Ham and Swiss Pierogi *(page 46)*

Ukrainian Meatballs *(page 70)*

Fried Fish Sandwiches *(page 203)*

Potato Pancakes *(page 100)*

Black and White Cookies *(page 114)*

GLOSSARY

Allspice berries can be purchased whole or ground. They are the unripe berries of a tropical tree.

Aspic is a savory jelly, usually made with stock and gelatin and always served chilled.

Bagels were initially a Jewish food, but they have become one of the emblematic foods of New York City. They are dense, chewy rings of bread that are boiled quickly before they are baked.

Barley, a very digestible grain, is often used in soup and also to make beer.

Bigos is a meat and cabbage stew that is cooked long and slow. It is eaten throughout Eastern Europe, but is most strongly connected with Poland.

Blintzes are thin pancakes similar to crepes. They are often filled with farmer's cheese and sometimes topped with fruit.

Borscht is an Eastern European soup that usually contains beets in some form or another. It may be served hot or cold.

Buckwheat flour is ground from buckwheat, which is not, as often assumed, a kind of grain but is instead a grass.

Cake flour is made from softer wheat than all-purpose flour. It gives cakes and other baked goods a very tender crumb.

Cardamom is made by grinding the seeds of a plant in the ginger family.

Challah is a leavened egg bread of Jewish origin. For religious purposes, challah is formed into a braid and then baked for the Sabbath. At Veselka we shape our nondenominational bread into a Pullman loaf for sandwiches.

Ciabatta is the Italian word for "slipper," but it also refers to a kind of white bread with a lot of holes in the crumb. At Veselka, we use ciabatta rolls for several of our sandwiches.

Cumin is sold ground or in whole seeds. It is derived from a plant similar to parsley.

Durum flour is made from durum wheat, which is harder (i.e., has a higher protein content) than the wheat used to make all-purpose flour. Durum flour, sometimes called semolina flour, is used to make pasta.

European-style butter contains more butterfat than regular butter (about 82% or 83% as opposed to 80%). It also contains less moisture, which makes for richer pastries.

Farmer's cheese looks like a drier version of cottage cheese and, indeed, can be replaced with drained cottage cheese in a pinch. It is a mild cheese with visible curds.

Fondant is a premade sugar paste, which can easily be rolled out (like a dough) and cut into various shapes. It is also easy to color.

Frangipane is a sweet almond mixture used as a filling in pies and tarts.

Herring is a small cold-water fish that is on the oily side.

Holubtsi is a Ukrainian word meaning "little pigeons," but also referring to a dish of stuffed cabbage, presumably because the little packets of cabbage wedged together in a baking dish resemble sleeping birds.

Kasha is the Russian word for buckwheat groats, which are available whole or in fine, medium, or large "grinds."

Kielbasa is the Polish name for what in Ukrainian is korbasa, a smoked pork sausage (sometimes made with beef, too) that is eaten throughout Eastern Europe.

Kutya is a kind of poppy seed and wheat berry porridge that is a ritual Christmas dish in Ukraine.

Panko bread crumbs are unseasoned and very dry. They provide an extra-crispy crust.

Paprika is commonly used in Eastern European cooking. The spice is made by grinding dried peppers.

Pierogi are stuffed dumplings. Pierogi is usually the Polish word for what in Ukrainian are known as pyrohy, but pierogi is the more commonly used word in the United States, as well as the word we use on Veselka's menu, so that's what we've called them here, too.

Uzvar is the fruit compote always eaten as part of the Christmas meal in Ukraine.

Varenyky is another name for pierogi.

Veselka is the Ukrainian word for "rainbow."

Vushka are small dumplings. The word literally means "little ears" in Ukrainian, as the filled dumplings resemble ears in shape.

RESOURCES

FARMERS' MARKETS

Farmers' markets are a fantastic resource for fruits and vegetables, but also for local meat, poultry, and fish, cheeses, honey, plants, and just about anything else. If you live in New York City, you probably already know about the Greenmarket network: This is comprised of 45 different farmers' markets around the city. The largest one is in Union Square, not far from Veselka, four days a week, but there is also a smaller market one block from Veselka in front of St. Mark's Church on Tuesdays. Locust Grove Farm in Ulster County is one of the farms that sells produce there (as well as in Union Square twice a week), and we have purchased apples and other fruit from them for years. (They've been with the Greenmarket since it was founded in 1976.) It's part of our philosophy of using top-notch ingredients, and everything they sell is delicious. To learn more about New York City Greenmarkets, visit www.cenyc.org/greenmarket. And if you live in another area, look for a farmers' market near you. I guarantee you'll be glad you did.

BREAD

You can get good bread almost anywhere in the country these days, and you can even make your own (see pages 185–88), but at Veselka we purchase a lot of our bread from Amy's Bread. Owner Amy Scherber is one of the American bakers behind the bread renaissance in this country in recent years. Amy's Bread has three locations in New York City: one in Hell's Kitchen, one in Chelsea Market, and one on Bleecker Street in Greenwich Village. Visit www.amysbread.com for more information.

BUFFALO MEAT

Buffalo meat is increasingly popular because it offers a high protein content with less fat than beef from cows. It is probably available in your local grocery store, but you may not have noticed it in the butcher's case if you were not looking for it. There is at least one purveyor who sells buffalo meat at the Greenmarkets, New York City's farmers' markets (see above). If you cannot find ground buffalo meat to make Buffalo Burgers (page 200) in your area, you can easily order it online. One good company is The Buffalo Guys (www.thebuffaloguys.com or 1-888-330-8686) in Wyoming. Wild Idea Buffalo Company (www.wildideabuffalo.com or 1-866-658-6137) is also a reliable source.

CHEDDAR CHEESE

Our preferred cheddar cheese is from Cabot Creamery in Vermont. Their cheddar cheese is prizewinning, and aside from finding an artisanal cheesemaker in your area, they are your best bet for consistently good cheddar. You can find a store near you that carries their excellent cheddar at their Web site, www.cabotcheese.com.

CHIPOTLE PEPPERS IN ADOBO SAUCE

These peppers wield a delicious smoky kick. They can be found on many grocery store shelves, usually in the "ethnic" section, as they are considered a Latin ingredient.

FARMER'S CHEESE

Farmer's cheese is widely available in grocery stores. It's a moist, mild, fresh (not aged) cheese that comes in a tub. If you can't locate farmer's cheese near you, you can make a close facsimile by draining some cottage cheese in a coffee filter placed in a strainer. Set the strainer over a bowl and refrigerate overnight. Because cottage cheese has larger curds than farmer's cheese, whip the resulting cheese with a fork or whisk before proceeding with the recipe.

FONDANT

Fondant is simply sugar and water cooked and then beaten to a creamy consistency. It makes a stable covering for confections, and we use it to frost our Black and White Cookies (page 114). You can find fondant at baking and cake decorating stores. One excellent store is New York Cake and Baking Distributors at 56 West 22nd Street in the Flatiron district, www

.nycake.com or 800-942-2539. King Arthur Flour (see Specialty Flours on page 248) also sells fondant in two-pound buckets.

KASHA

Wolff's is the only brand of kasha (buckwheat groats) I've ever seen in a supermarket, and it's the kind we use at Veselka as well. If you have trouble finding it in your area, you can always order it directly from the company at www.wolffskasha.com.

KIELBASA

Forty years ago, when I was just starting to work at Veselka, the neighborhood was distinctly and markedly Ukrainian. There were several Ukrainian butchers that made their own kielbasa and sold other Ukrainian favorites. Those days are gone. We're very lucky that Baczynsky's (also known as the East Village Meat Market) continues to flourish. Not only do we buy our kielbasa and other meat from them, but they also smoke the turkey breasts for our turkey sandwiches. (See page 67 for more on the long-standing relationship between Veselka and Baczynsky's.) It is definitely worth a visit if you are in New York, and Baczynsky's does mail order business, but only during cool weather. We also buy our smoked pork ribs and ham hocks for White Borscht (page 16) there.

East Village Meat Market (aka Baczynsky's)
139 Second Avenue between St. Mark's Place and 9th Street
212-228-5590

The next best thing is to find a butcher in your area that makes its own kielbasa. Barring that, you might try ordering kielbasa online from a place such as Kacer's (www.kacerkielbossa .com) or Fil's Deli (www.filspolishdeli.com). The industrially made sausage that is labeled kielbasa and sold in the supermarket would be my last choice, to be used only in an emergency.

PANKO BREAD CRUMBS

Panko are a particularly dry, fine type of bread crumb that comes from Japan. For most recipes in this book, regular breadcrumbs will do, but for breading a chicken breast, we find that panko are best. They are increasingly available in mainstream grocery stores (check the ethnic foods section) and, of course, Asian grocery stores. Right around the corner from Veselka, on East 9th Street between Third and Second Avenues, there is a small Japanese grocery store, Sunrise Mart, that carries several different brands of panko. They are available on-line at myriad Web sites.

SAUERKRAUT

We highly recommend making your own sauerkraut using the recipe on page 94. It's surprisingly simple, and you will taste a huge difference. Even then, though, you will need a batch of "starter" sauerkraut. Do seek out artisanal sauerkraut rather than the industrial type. It tastes of cabbage and doesn't have any artificial preservatives or cultures. The sauerkraut from Hawthorne Valley Farm (www.hawthornevalleyfarm.org or 518-672-7500) is recommended by Slow Food, an organization dedicated to recognizing foods made the old-fashioned way. Hawthorne Valley Farm is present at the Greenmarkets (see above) and also sells via mail order.

SMOKED SALMON AND SALT-PRESERVED HERRING

At Veselka, we serve smoked salmon from Catsmo, a company in the Catskill mountains of New York state that smokes salmon in small batches. Catsmo has a Web site (www.catsmo .com), but doesn't sell its products retail. You could contact them and ask for a list of stores that stock Catsmo smoked salmon if you like. We're very lucky in New York to have several excellent "appetizing stores," such as Russ & Daughters at 179 East Houston Street, that sell smoked fish of all kinds and styles. If you are not quite so lucky where you live, Russ & Daughters has a Web site (www.russanddaughters.com) or you can call them at 1-800-RUSS-229 (212-475-4880 in the tri-state area). They are happy to ship orders and also sell babka, bagels, and excellent dried fruit and nuts.

SPECIALTY FLOURS AND WHEAT BERRIES

Specialty flours such as bread flour and durum flour can often be found in mainstream grocery stores, but a great resource for flours and baking equipment is the King Arthur Flour catalogue, www.kingarthurflour.com. King Arthur also carries wheat berries for making Kutya (page 163). Wheat berries are available in health food stores, and they often appear on grocery store shelves (sometimes cooked and in jars) around Easter, as they are an ingredient in traditional Italian Easter pastries.

SPICES

What a different world we live in than even just a few years ago. While at one time spices such as paprika and allspice berries were unusual, today they're commonplace on grocery store shelves. However, high turnover is important. Spices don't go bad, exactly, but they do lose flavor and potency as they age. Penzeys Spices (www.penzeys.com) is a great on-line catalogue and offers just about everything under the sun.

WAFFLE FLOUR

Our recipe for Buttermilk Waffles is simple enough, but at the restaurant we buy waffle flour in large quantities from Carbon's for convenience. Carbon's sells all kinds of pancake and waffle flour, including malted and flavored varieties. They also sell KitchenAid and VillaWare waffle irons.

Carbon's Golden Malted
www.newcarbon.com
1-800-253-0590

UKRAINIAN INFORMATION

The Web site www.brama.com serves as a kind of clearinghouse for all things Ukrainian in the United States. The Ukrainian Institute of America also has a useful Web site, www.ukrainian institute.org.

INDEX